Always in the search

3.xi.2016

"An unforgettable saga of determination, strength, sacrifice, and love set against the background of unspeakable horrors during World War II in the Pacific Ocean Theater."

GILBERT KING, author of the Pulitzer Prize-winning *Devil in the Grove: Thurgood Marshall, the Groveland Boys, and the Dawn of a New America*

"Minter Dial's grandson, named for him, has spent years of his own life tracking down facts and shaping them into *The Last Ring Home*, a story of the human costs of war, life and death, love and loss."

GAVAN DAWS, author of *Prisoners of the Japanese: POWs of World War II in the Pacific*

"Minter Dial spent decades piecing together the life of the grandfather he never knew, in a quest that plunged him deep into one of the darkest chapters of the Pacific War. *The Last Ring Home* is the unforgettable story he uncovered—a tale of bravery, brutality, and monumental suffering. This book is a loving testimonial to the sacrifices of an entire generation."

JANNY SCOTT, author of *A Singular Woman: The Untold Story of Barack Obama's Mother*

"Here is an inspired feat of historical sleuthing that stretches across generations and continents. In this feelingly told account of the heroic life of a grandfather he never knew, Minter Dial reminds us that history, above all else, is personal."

"The legacy of the Americans who surrendered after the 1942 Battle of the Philippines can now add a new voice. *The Last Ring Home* is a poignant story of suffering and loss across the generations ... and one U.S. Naval Academy ring, which will leave readers thinking about the endurance of tenderness."

"Minter Dial has, with remarkable success, blended intimate family history with one of the more horrifying aspects of the Second World War. He vividly captures the unimaginable ordeal endured by his namesake grandfather. The result is a stark presentation of the sufferings and hopes of a young man caught up in a manmade manifestation of Hell."

— The Last Ring Home —

MINTER DIAL II

A POW's Lasting Legacy
of Courage, Love, and
Honor in World War II

The

LAST RING

HOME

mindset
PRESS

Myndset Press
thelastringhome.com

ISBN 978-0-9955006-0-0 (hardcover)
ISBN 978-0-9955006-1-7 (ebook)

Jacket and text design by Peter Cocking
Photographs courtesy of Diana Dial
Editing by Helen Reeves and Kristen Steenbeeke
Proofing by Lucy Kenward
Printed and bound in Canada by Friesens
Distributed in North America by Midpoint Trade Books
and in the United Kingdom and Europe by Gazelle

16 17 18 19 20   5 4 3 2 1

Oft, as in airy rings they skim the heath,
The clam'rous lapwings feel the leaden death;
Oft, as the mounting larks their notes prepare,
They fall and leave their little lives in air.

"WINDSOR FOREST"
ALEXANDER POPE · 1713

Bright is the ring of words
When the right man rings them.

"BRIGHT IS THE RING OF WORDS"
ROBERT LOUIS STEVENSON · 1895

The ring, so worn as you behold,
So thin, so pale, is yet of gold.

"A MARRIAGE RING"
GEORGE CRABBE · 1813–1814

— Contents —

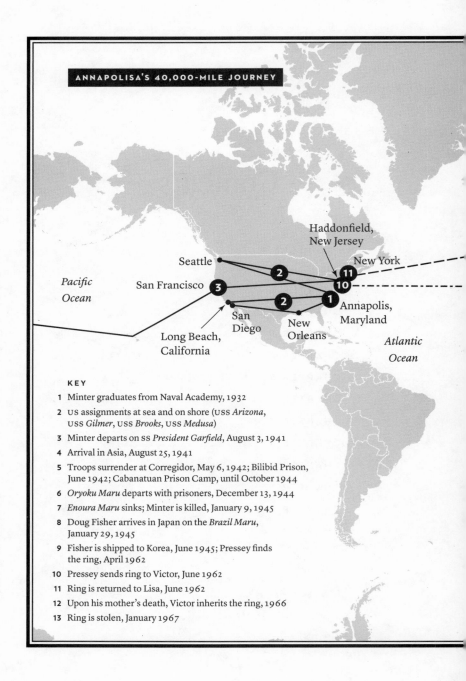

ANNAPOLISA'S 40,000-MILE JOURNEY

Haddonfield, New Jersey

Seattle

New York

Pacific Ocean

San Francisco **3**

2

11
10

2

1 Annapolis, Maryland

San Diego

New Orleans

Long Beach, California

Atlantic Ocean

KEY

1 Minter graduates from Naval Academy, 1932

2 US assignments at sea and on shore (USS *Arizona*, USS *Gilmer*, USS *Brooks*, USS *Medusa*)

3 Minter departs on SS *President Garfield*, August 3, 1941

4 Arrival in Asia, August 25, 1941

5 Troops surrender at Corregidor, May 6, 1942; Bilibid Prison, June 1942; Cabanatuan Prison Camp, until October 1944

6 *Oryoku Maru* departs with prisoners, December 13, 1944

7 *Enoura Maru* sinks; Minter is killed, January 9, 1945

8 Doug Fisher arrives in Japan on the *Brazil Maru*, January 29, 1945

9 Fisher is shipped to Korea, June 1945; Pressey finds the ring, April 1962

10 Pressey sends ring to Victor, June 1962

11 Ring is returned to Lisa, June 1962

12 Upon his mother's death, Victor inherits the ring, 1966

13 Ring is stolen, January 1967

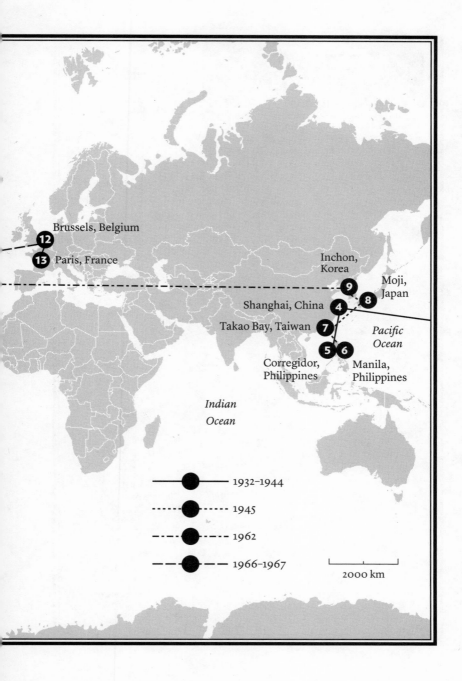

Brussels, Belgium
12
13 Paris, France

Inchon, Korea
9
Moji, Japan
8
Shanghai, China **4**
Takao Bay, Taiwan **7**
5 **6**
Pacific Ocean
Corregidor, Philippines
Manila, Philippines

Indian Ocean

● —— 1932–1944
● ······ 1945
● —·—·— 1962
● — — — 1966–1967

2000 km

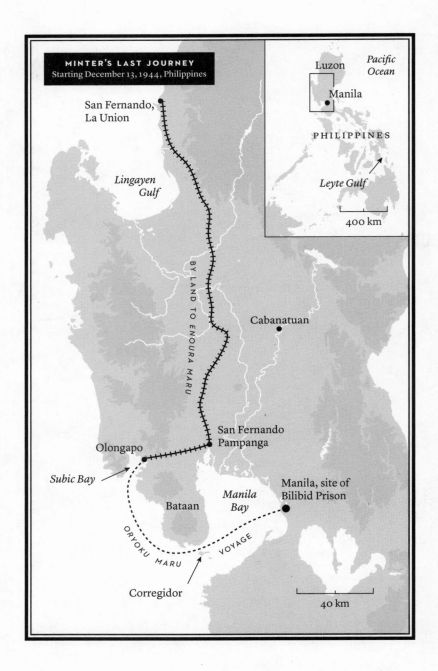

— Prologue —

ARRYING THE NAME of another, much less a moniker
such as Nathaniel Minter Dial, is a bit of a weight. As the
grandson of a true war hero, the family name came with
even more heft than usual, and yet I was a fully grown man before
I delved into the story of my grandfather and namesake. Named
Nathaniel for his father and Minter after his mother's maiden
name, the original Nathaniel Minter Dial carried even in his name
the proud traditions and typically high expectations of his Southern ancestors.

By the time of my birth in 1964, Minter, my grandfather, and
Lisa, his wife and my grandmother, were both dead. The only
grandparent I had known on my father's side was my stepgrand-
father, Kennett Webb Hinks (who you will meet in this story). He
was the most wonderful of men: caring, gregarious, and a partner
in some of the perfect memories I had growing up—including one
summer on a dude ranch in Wyoming, racing across the prairie on
horseback and camping under the stars. He mesmerized me with
stories (and had plenty to spare as a former chief of planning with
the Office of Strategic Services, the predecessor to today's CIA)
and made me a devotee for life by loaning me his 1955 turquoise
convertible Thunderbird when I was old enough to drive. With

such a grandfather, who needed to blow the dust off an old legend and investigate one's real grandfather?

Apparently, I did.

It started with a call I received in December of 1991. After spending most of my life in Europe, I had just moved to Washington, DC, four months prior, when a woman representing Western High School in the District phoned me.

"Is this Nathaniel Dial?"

"Yes," I said, "although they refer to me as Minter."

"Oh yes, I see that's your middle name."

"May I ask what you are calling about?"

"My name is Mrs. Ellie Chucker, class of 1951. You see, I want to invite you to your school reunion."

"Really? Which one might that be? I went to a whole lot of schools."

"Western High School, although now it's called the Duke Ellington School for the Arts. Back in your days, sir, it was called Western High School."

"That's most peculiar," I suggested.

"Why's that?"

"Because I didn't go to any Western School."

"But you are Nathaniel *Minter* Dial?"

"I am."

Silence.

"The funny thing is, you sound rather young," Mrs. Chucker admitted.

Mildly put off, I countered that I was much closer to thirty than twenty, quietly wondering if that qualified me as old. After a pause, Mrs. Chucker explained that the man she was looking for would have been in his eighties.

It was only then that it dawned on me that she was looking for my grandfather, after whom I had been named.

This was an immense surprise for both of us. For Mrs. Chucker, when she came across my name in the newspaper, she felt sure that the "N M Dial" she had come across in the classifieds *had* to be the same person. Especially when she was able to confirm that the N and M stood for the same names. She just kept repeating, "I'll be darned." I could hear her shaking her head.

After a few minutes of explanation, I came to understand that my grandfather had gone to high school in Washington from 1924 to 1928, and that the current version of the school was inviting back its oldest alumni for a series of reunions. The program to regroup the alumni was just three years old in 1991. In the case of my grandfather, they were working on the fifty-fifth reunion. Mrs. Chucker had the records of nine living classmates.

For myself, this was at once a mysterious gift and a call to action. I immediately (and illogically) felt as if I had been put in touch with my grandfather. Also, I was now, for the very first time in my life, made aware of his existence. Up until that point, he had been an abstract person. Sure, I knew I had been named after him, but all I knew was that he had died in the war. And, to be sure, I hadn't even thought much about that, since he had died in a part of the war I had never studied. At school in England, my focus had always been the European theater. Even my father, Minter's son, had never spoken much of his father, presumably since he had left for the war when my father was just three years old and his sister, Diana, only a baby. I assumed they also knew very little about him.

Not wanting to let the occasion slip, I asked if I could get into contact directly with the other surviving classmates. She assured me that she would send me a list with their names and addresses. My only thought then was not to waste this fortuitous opportunity. I didn't know what would come of it and didn't call my father or aunt at this time. I only planned to write a few letters. I had no idea what I was getting myself into.

A week or so later, I received a manila envelope with a list printed out on white dot matrix printer paper. Various names had been crossed out or had been marked "deceased." My grandfather's name had been newly crossed off.

I then fired off handwritten letters over the course of the next few days. It took about a fortnight to get my first letter back. From the nine men to whom I had written, I received eight letters back. Some were rather cursory and apologetic for not remembering anything in particular about my grandfather. A few were considerably longer, augmented by the fact that they had gone on to Annapolis as well and thus had been classmates for four more years. In one case, Minter had ended up staying in touch for most of the rest of his life.

Since my aunt Diana lived in Washington, I saw a good deal more of her than I saw either my father (who was living in France) or mother (in Philadelphia). But, as with my father, as I recall it, my aunt didn't seem hungry to find out about the content of any of the letters. I didn't ask why, but continued with my research— since by now that was what it had become. With those first letters, my search into what type of man my grandfather was, what he lived through, and how he ultimately died began.

It wasn't always easy and certainly never pretty, but the hunt was endlessly fascinating. I spoke to old veterans and their wives, read hundreds of their letters, and dug up old memories with children and grandchildren of those who lived through the war. I combed through war records, read as many books as I could muster that dealt with this part of the war in search of any references, and received help from scores of librarians and war historians, including immeasurable assistance from the staff at the US Naval Academy. In doing so, I brought back some painful feelings for those in my own family—whose gracious help I could not have done without and for which I will be ever grateful.

What the search stirred in me was most surprising: a feeling of pride for sharing the blood of such a valiant man; a terrible sadness about so much promise lost and an empathy for the pain my grandmother, Lisa, bore; a deep burning anger about the inhumanity of war; and, oddly, a guilt that I, who have never had to fight, could live with such ease, laugh without restraint, and enjoy my life with a sense of freedom hard purchased by those men who died in battle. Today, I feel as though I owe them something—recognition and respect, at least. I hope this book serves to settle some of that debt.

I must point out here that many facts about the war in the Philippines—such as the Bataan Death March, the POW camps, and the Japanese hell ships—are disputed, even by those who survived them. Casualty numbers vary, as do troop strengths, the chronology of events, and practically all other information. Records are missing or incomplete, and old soldiers' memories fade. I have tried to find the reliable facts, based on official Navy records, war crime tribunal court documents, and the like; but I am sure there are inaccuracies, and I welcome contradictory information. Also, I have filled in the known facts of this biography with some assumptions about what *might* have happened, based on interviews with those still living and letters from those no longer with us. I have also made use of the research of many of the wonderful historians who have covered this subject matter before me, and I mention their important and informative books in the list of references in the endnotes. I urge you to read them if you are at all interested in the dramatic events and astonishing bravery displayed by the Allied troops in the Philippines during World War II. It's a part of WWII that is not widely known or covered in classrooms. May this book help us never to forget what happened there.

Above all, I owe thanks to the most special person in my life, my wife, Yendi. During the (long) period of writing this book, she graced me with the patience, encouragement, and advice that powered me through early-morning pre-work hours of writing and reading. She is the star that guides all my efforts.

Researching the story of my grandfather and his ring led me not only to come to understand him and his journey, but also taught me much about myself and my own journey. Whether it was coping with being in New York when the Twin Towers came down on September 11, 2001, and in Paris for the bombings on

November 13, 2015, or just dealing with all my daily stresses and problems, the deeper knowledge of what my grandfather and all members of the Greatest Generation experienced has been a source of great inspiration.

Some of the serendipitous events that sprang from the story helped make me, though not a religious man, a more spiritual and fulfilled one. I felt throughout as though the spirit of my grandfather was leading me onward. For this, I thank him—Minter Dial, athlete, *pater familias*, warrior, and my hero. I am very glad I finally got to know him.

– 1 –

HE CROUCHED ON his cracked heels above the dirt floor, the shreds of his uniform stuck between his thighs by weeks of sweat and grime. He could no longer smell himself or anybody else in the hut. Good thing. Slavery stank.

The dysentery rampant among the men didn't help matters. Poor bastards. Minter knew how they felt—cramping as their guts twisted, a knife-like pain deep in their bowels, followed by the helplessness that came when the diarrhea couldn't be stopped. It was humiliating, he remembered. He had just recovered from pneumonia when they first brought him to this hellhole, his body too weak to fight off the camp curse. At the time, Minter had found himself apologizing to the other guys for what he couldn't control. Now, he no longer apologized for things like that. There wasn't much here any of them could control.

There were no good days, but there were some days not as bad as others. Today wasn't one of those. He held his head, feeling the grit burrow into the sunburnt cracks of his forehead and the strips of skin that came off in his hand.

I am rotting, he thought. My body is rotting away right into the muck of this godforsaken jungle. What is left of me, the flies will eat.

He looked over at one of his buddies, asleep with his mouth open. Flies were using it as a landing pad. Who knew there were this many types of flies? Blue flies, black flies, horse flies, and maggots in everything, hatching new flies.

Jesus, snap out of it, he told himself. Chin up, chin up, chin up, chinup, chinup, chinupchinup, he said faster and faster, slapping his own face. Think of something else.

He tried to turn his thoughts to Lisa and his kids, but the thought faded like a mirage in the desert. His mouth felt beyond parched, as though all moisture had fled forever, replaced by a vile-tasting film coating his tongue and teeth. A couple of scoops of rice a day didn't cut it and there was never enough water—or the brackish, warm swill that passed for water. He would kill for an ice-cold beer.

That thought started the flood of images: drinking frosty mint juleps in silver cups, so cold the condensation ran down the side; flipping cheeseburgers on the backyard grill; three-scoop banana splits with extra whipped cream; huge rare T-bone steaks with thick strips of fat, dished up with sautéed Vidalia onions. His stomach grumbled in never-ending complaint.

He knew he was obsessed with food. They all were. At night, the men would call to each other in the darkness. Strawberry rhubarb pie. Georgia peaches. Asparagus with hollandaise sauce. Everyone would groan; but the voices went on—reciting recipes for mashed potatoes with whole sticks of butter or New England clam chowder full of cream and carrots. They planned elaborate menus for the meals they would eat when they got home. On and on the talk of food would go until exhaustion took over and they finally passed out.

The next morning, the sun would rise again, starting its climb into a cloudless sky. He would pull himself out of his bunk, already feeling the heat of the day, and use up more of his waning strength to do mule labor for his captors, hoping that soon he and the other men could go home. He did his part, but resentment boiled in him.

That fire had been stoked when he'd read the circular being passed around. In it, the camp's American commanding officer, Colonel Curtis Beecher, had written,

"However lowly and humble our present position, we are fortunate in being assembled here alive and more or less physically fit. I desire to impress upon you that we are operating under a strictly absolute power. There is only one interpretation, and that is the Japanese interpretation. The Japanese make all the decisions.... Ours is a state of complete subjugation. Your duty is to obey."[1]

Screw that, he thought.

He untied the heavy gold ring from the fabric shred around his waist that concealed it. He kept it there, except when the Japs were around, and then, like the other men, he'd unclench his shriveled buttocks and hide the ring inside his own body. The ring now hung so loosely he could wear it on his index finger. He twirled it around, letting the blue stone catch a random ray of sun shining through the thatched roof. *Annapolis, Class of 1932.* Only ten years, but a lifetime ago.

He remembered the night he and his classmates had baptized the ring in a bowl containing the waters of the seven seas during a ritual passed on from class to class.[2] He thought of how hard he had worked and what fun he'd had with his buddies. Staying up all night cramming for exams. Horsing around in the dorms. Sunbathing on Macdonough Beach. Putting war paint on that old bust of Tecumseh. Being herded to chapel by the Hellcats (where he had sometimes gone back later and slipped in to pray). Working as a team at the lacrosse games. Learning to keep faith with your buddy and to always have your shipmate's back. Being made to understand that commitment to the service was an honor, not just a duty, and that valor was an action word.

His time at the Academy had shaped him and had made him a man. At graduation, when he had earned the right to turn the ring to face his heart, he had joined a brotherhood—one that would be unbroken even by death.[3]

Generations of Navy men had demonstrated steadfastness and bravery. Now it was his time to carry on that tradition.

True, this particular generation was fighting a war against foreign enemies who seemed intent on reducing all those they captured to beasts, not men. In this war, at this time, the brotherhood was a special lot, a subset of a subset of bad fortune, an elite of the damned.[4] But they would hold their heads up, dig deep to hang onto their spirits and, if it were possible, they would survive this nightmare and join the ranks of Navy men who had served their country with honor. The ring symbolized all of that to him. He would wear it proudly forever if he lived, and, if he didn't, one of his buddies would survive to take it back home for his wife to have and to pass on to his son, a permanent reminder of his father's love.

He'd seen a Jap guard try to wrench such a ring from another prisoner's swollen knuckle. When the ring wouldn't come off, the guard swung his sword and took it off—finger and all. Lt. Minter Dial, USN, swore right there that his ring would make it through this damn war.

He hoped he'd be alive to wear it.

— 2 —

B Y THE TIME I stumbled into this project at age twenty-
seven, I had moved countries five times and had lived at
a total of fifteen addresses. I was an American citizen, but
a rather itinerant one. I certainly felt more European in upbring-
ing, having been born in Brussels and lived outside of America
for my first eighteen years. To say that I had a pat answer to the
question "Where do you come from?" would have been entirely
inaccurate.

My life came in stark contrast to my grandfather's lineage.
Both the Minters and the Dials likely considered themselves to be
Americans second, Southerners first. On top of that, Minter's heritage was one of distinct and important public service. His paternal
grandfather, Albert Dial, had been a well-regarded captain during
the Civil War. His great uncle had been the young and highly dec-
orated Gen. Dodson Ramseur. Not least, his father was a senator.
Minter Dial learned early what was expected of him—whether the
expectations were stated openly or not.

The first of these lessons had to do with being a "Southern
Gentleman," a sobriquet so ingrained in the generations that pre-
ceded young Minter that it led to the firm belief, held by many, that
the Confederacy would surely win the Civil War. This assumption

was based largely on the fact that they were gentlemen and the Yankees were barbarians.

In commemorating the way of life the Southerners had lived for generations, author Margaret Mitchell wrote, "Here was a land of cavaliers and cotton fields called the Old South. Here, in this pretty world, gallantry took its last bow. Here was the last ever to be seen of knights and their ladies fair; of master and of slave. Look for it only in books, for it is no more than a dream remembered. A civilization gone with the wind."[1]

But one needn't rely on fiction to understand how the Southern man viewed himself. In an editorial published at the beginning of the Civil War, a resident of the Dial family's own state wrote,

> "The South Carolinians are among the most sagacious and practical of mankind, a people of great self-denial and self-control, grave and decorous in their courtesies as the grandees of old Spain, and as fleece and invincible in war as the Zouaves of that France whose blood flows freely in their veins."[2]

Such fierce pride came with high expectations, and these were passed down as a code of honor among men of the South (and are so to this present day), especially to the sons of the upper classes. To whom much was given, much was expected. *Noblesse oblige* and service to one's country were as much a part of the Southern culture as chivalry and defense of personal honor.

An inscription on a monument in Ellaville, Georgia, eulogizes the Confederate soldiers as having "lived true to every honorable tradition that illuminates the pages of our history, and at the call of duty laid down their lives. A noble sacrifice on the altar of their country."[3]

Minter's own father, Nathaniel Barksdale Dial, was born two years before the end of what he surely had learned was the "War of Northern Aggression" and grew up in the shadow of the Glorious (and lost) Cause.

His father, Capt. Albert Dial, had served during the war under the legendary Robert E. Lee. Lee's army idolized him and fought nearly to the last man for him. Captain Dial no doubt instilled in his son some of the values Lee and the Cause had inspired in him.

General Lee had high expectations of his soldiers, saying, "Duty is the sublimest word in our language. Do your duty in all things. You cannot do more. You should never wish to do less."[4]

Captain Dial expected as much from his son.

Nathaniel Barksdale Dial was exposed to another part of being a proper Southern Gentleman. The slaves his father owned worked the family's plantation in Laurens, South Carolina. Manual labor was not expected of young Nathaniel, but the idea of devoting oneself to something larger was.

Nathaniel decided to pursue a career in law. After obtaining an undergraduate degree at Vanderbilt University, he studied law at the University of Virginia, passed the bar in 1883, and by 1887 had become part of something larger by running for and winning the office of mayor of Laurens. It was his first foray into public service. He served three terms as mayor. However, he declined the office of consul to Zurich, Switzerland, tendered by President Grover Cleveland in 1893, presumably because he preferred to stay in the thick of his local activities and in the comfort of Southern hospitality.

During these years, he also took a wife, Ruth Mitchell, who, after twenty years of marriage and six children, died after a sudden illness.[5] The forty-four-year-old widower then married Josephine (Josie or Jou-Jou) Minter, literally the girl next door.

"Many a note of endearment passed across the alley, as well as flowers and fresh fruits from Nathaniel's garden and vineyards. With difficulty, Josephine restrained from impulse to flash in public Nathaniel's solitaire ... due to her stepmother's recent death, she wished to have as little publicity and fanfare as possible."[6]

In the Minters' candlelit living room, with members of the two families and their closest friends on hand, the couple took their vows. The wedding march was played on Josephine's Steinway concert grand; a radiantly happy bride wore Nathaniel's wedding gift—a diamond sunburst.[7]

Nathaniel was, by all reports, a good family man and husband, playing the archetypical Southern patriarch to his growing brood and coddling his new bride—demonstrating another way in which a Southern Gentleman behaved.[8] He was also a prominent businessman with a variety of interests, including three banks, several power companies, a textile company, a glass foundry, a bus company, and a health resort.[9]

In an age when women did not work outside the home and were expected to devote themselves to God, their husband, their children, and their charities (in that order), Josephine had a noticeable artistic bent. Neighborhood gossips thought she would be wasting herself on that "Nat Dial with his gang of children." But soon, Nathaniel donned a frock coat and added to his cultural *bona fides* by accompanying Jou-Jou on visits to music and art festivals.[10]

Such conviviality soon led to Nathaniel and Josephine adding to their family. Minter (Nathaniel Minter Dial) was born in 1911, and, along with his three other siblings, Fannie, Dorothy, and Joseph, joined the remaining four children (two others had died in infancy) from the previous marriage.

They were children of privilege even in their rural setting. Their large brick home had been designed by the architect Allen L. Melton, who also designed the famed Biltmore House in Asheville, North Carolina. The Dial children had a fully equipped playground, woodlands, and a meadow, complete with a running creek (where a young Minter spent hours fashioning sculptures from the clay banks) as well as their own servant, Tobey, who was a natural storyteller.

Josephine set a fine table, using her wedding silver and bone china, and guests such as Nathaniel's business associates and local celebrities all dined by the light of grand banquet candelabras.[11] The Dials also spent time entertaining Nathaniel's huge cast of relatives, including forty-five first cousins. The couple became known for their parties and their dancing, earning them the title "The Dancing Dials." Young Minter was taught good manners and held to a strict discipline, reinforcing the dictum that Southern boys were expected to become gentlemen—gracious to all.

Such social polish would come in handy for his father as well, as Nathaniel had set his sights on public office. He ran for a seat in the state legislature in 1907, but had to withdraw when he contracted typhoid fever. For the state's senate seat in 1912, he took on incumbent Ben Tillman, who had been eighteen years in office, and lost. But, due partly to Tillman's fading health and the enthusiastic backing of President Wilson, Nathaniel finally won the senatorial seat in 1918, becoming the United States senator for South Carolina.

The Dials were going to Washington.

THE DISTRICT OF Columbia after WWI was a place of contrasts. Ninety-thousand mostly Southern African Americans had immigrated to the city after the Civil War. This led to housing shortages and the development of "blind alleys," which housed poor blacks and some whites in abominable circumstances behind the fine residences on Capitol Hill. The president's wife, Ellen Wilson, campaigned with social reformers to pass a congressional bill to abolish the alleys as residences. The bill finally passed in 1917, but a congressional mandate to eliminate the alley residences wasn't passed until 1944. As the new Senator Dial was soon to learn, things moved slowly, if at all, in the halls of Congress.

On the other side of town, the Dial family was settling into their grand new residence on Kalorama Triangle, in a neighborhood so prestigious that its stunning residences now make up DC's Embassy Row. Their neighbors were Captain and Mrs. Arthur McArthur, brother to the soon-to-be legendary general; Admiral and Mrs. William DuBose; and Attorney General Robert Lovett.

There was a complete African American staff to help Josephine run the house, and she entertained as befit her husband's new station. There were luncheons for the senators' wives, as well as parties, cotillions, and receptions. The children's photographs were taken for the society columns of the local magazines—Minter looking tall, solemn, and very well-scrubbed. Like all upper-class young men of his generation, Minter was sent to dancing school (a talent that never left him, as he was described by his sister later in life as "one who danced on air").

Meanwhile, Senator Dial was shown into his new office, given an orientation tour of the Senate Chamber, and prepared to add his voice to the Sixty-sixth United States Congress, which convened March 4, 1919, and ran until March 4, 1921, the last two years of Woodrow Wilson's presidency.[12]

The newly elected Senator Dial took his place in the Senate Chamber at his desk, perhaps one of the original forty-eight first made by cabinetmaker Thomas Constantine to replace those burnt when the British torched the Capitol in 1814. Senator Dial's desk, like his fellow senators', was small and made of mahogany, with a traditional inkwell, sander, and tray (though these implements were already outdated since the invention of the fountain pen). The chair had "red morocco leather seats to confer an image of power and authority," but, in fact, the Chamber itself helped negate that impression.[13] The lack of air circulation contributed to the premature deaths of thirty-four senators, according to physician (and future senator) Royal Copeland.[14] Because of poor acoustics, no one could hear clearly. Senator Dial could have taken that last fact as a sign.

He had fought hard to get to the Senate in order to walk in the footsteps of such Southern firebrands as South Carolina's fabled orator John C. Calhoun or Kentucky's Henry Clay, but instead found himself ignored and powerless.[15] He was a freshman, unknown to most of his contemporaries, and committee assignments during his tenure reflected his lack of seniority: Cuban Relations, District of Columbia, National Banks, Commerce, Public Buildings and Grounds, and finally Post Offices and Post Roads.

During his term in the Senate, Nathaniel denounced corruption like political patronage and the sale of public offices wherever he saw it. He stood up for his constituents, cotton farmers, and small-business owners. He was a consistent opponent of federal spending, believing that individual states should look after themselves. He was considered stingy with regard to federal spending, believing it to be "antagonistic to paternalistic legislation."[16]

When a national railroad strike was threatened in 1923, he said this: "An autocracy of labor is just as distasteful to the people of this country as an autocracy of capital, and we are not going to allow either to... rule our government."[17]

But it seemed to Senator Dial that no one was listening. It must have galled him to appear so impotent in front of his son, Minter, who no doubt frequented the visitor gallery to watch his father and the Senate debate the great issues of the day.

While he might have heard his father's frustration when Senator Dial railed at his situation upon returning home, it is also true that Minter would have absorbed the lesson that a boy like him was expected to contribute to the greater good, to serve his country, and to fight for what he believed was right.

Senator Dial soon came to believe that his fighting for what he believed to be right didn't matter anyway. Nothing could ever get done in the tangle of Washington politics.

He gave his most passionate speech about the Senate's lethargy and immobility in 1924 while running for reelection, arguing a point we still commonly hear from Americans of all political leanings in an address that could just as easily be given today:

> "I'm thoroughly disgusted by the way the government in Washington 'works.' There is almost total partisanship, both on the right and the left... neither side talks to the other, and... the divide just seems to be getting worse.... Self-interest comes before the national interest. By self-interest I don't just mean the interest a representative may or may not have for

his constituents, I also mean the desire to hang onto his job and all of its salary and benefits. I find the whole thing pretty pathetic."[18]

Needless to say, Nathaniel lost his renomination bid, but even that didn't stop him from speaking his mind.

In January 1925, just before relinquishing his Senate office, the lame-duck Senator Dial rose on the floor of the House and spoke to a nearly empty chamber. He gave a speech pillorying his fellow Democrats, many of whom had also suffered defeat in the recent election:

The Democratic Party should stand for

"ordered liberty, local self-government, encouragement, and development of individual initiative, self-confidence, and ambition; for the sovereignty and dignity of the state; for the right of every law-abiding citizen to conduct his own business, personal, and family affairs on his own responsibility; for resistance to every increase of the power of the Federal government not absolutely necessary to stability and efficiency."

"The Democratic Party has suffered successive defeats because it has ceased to be Democratic. Like sheep, we have gone astray.... It is a mortifying, bitter truth that the quiet and close-thinking man in the White House [Coolidge] just elected ... is a better Democrat in many essentials, more in accord with the foundation principles of the Democratic party than many men who have obtained high and honourable places as ostensible Democrats.... Democrats [should] ... follow the high, straight, outspoken American democracy instead of some kind of shambling, bastard, shame-faced mixture of so-called democracy and alien-conceived socialism or bolshevism or hell-broth of all."

The upsurge of business after the Democratic defeat he interpreted as evidence that businessmen, "[t]he active, live people, those in actual contact with life who do things, are against us.... It is time for us Democrats here to be facing the music... either the people are wrong or we Democrats here in Congress who have made the record for our party... are wrong.... [T]he same ethics and rules of honor we observe in our personal conduct should govern us in politics.... We have incurred along with the sting of defeat the more bitter sting of contempt."

He further eviscerated his own party, saying:

"Some would transform the American into a capon, fattening and cackling and entirely contented fenced in a barnyard" whereas the true American is the "bird of freedom... fit to soar, daring to look in the very eye of the sun... with a beak and talons."[19]

His remarks generated outrage among the members of his own party, who read them in the *Congressional Record* and howled in protest. They demanded Senator Dial retract his remarks, disown them, and make a formal apology. The group bullied and pestered him until he agreed. His remarks were stricken from the *Congressional Record* and became unofficially referred to as "the speech that never was."[20]

FOR HIS PART, in his own juvenile way, Minter was transforming into the most perfect vision of himself he could conjure, no doubt to please his father, whom he respected, and his mother, whom he adored. He got consistently high grades in school and was thought by those around him to be respectful, kind, compassionate, considerate, courteous, trustworthy, reliable, and energetic.[21]

Minter was also partially a product of his time. He read every issue of *Boy's Life Magazine* ("How to build an igloo" and "What to do if you're lost") which preached self-reliance along with a strong dose of clean bodies, clean minds, and manly patriotism; avidly followed the Hardy Boys, two all-American boys who solved impossible mysteries with just their wits; and read all Edgar Rice Burroughs's books about Tarzan, who was ever the hero, with feats of derring-do displayed in the African jungle. Minter followed reports about Admiral Byrd's death-defying Antarctic expedition, Charles Lindbergh's heroic flight across the Atlantic, and, of course, learned many stories about the heroism of the troops in World War I. He was an Eagle Scout, and at age twelve he fashioned a bronze bust of President Wilson, which he sent to the former president. President Wilson sent back a letter thanking his "little friend," and Minter, once again, got his photo in the newspapers, but this time for his own achievement, not just as his father's son. He also got art lessons, courtesy of his mother, under the instruction of a prominent Washington sculptor.[22]

He was a boy raised to succeed and given every opportunity to do so. No doubt, Minter interpreted success as being a leader of men and a bit of a hero himself.

MINTER, THE EVER-EXEMPLARY student, graduated from Western High School in 1928, having been class treasurer and having served on the student council. He had also been a star on the varsity track and basketball teams.

He was tall, handsome, popular, athletic, and headed to the United States Naval Academy. One of his father's friends in the Senate had sponsored his application.

Minter Dial finally had a chance to make his mark in the world and prove his worth in the hall of men. He couldn't wait to get to Annapolis.

— 3 —

MY FATHER, VICTOR, has few memories or mementos of his father, but he carries a permanent reminder of one of Minter's dearest friends. William "Ruffin" Cox met Minter in Annapolis in July 1928, and the two soon formed a life-long bond, with Ruffin eventually becoming godfather to Minter's son. Victor recalls:

"I carry a scar just below the thumb of my left hand from a self-inflicted wound while carving the fuselage of a B-17 when I was five. The knife slipped and made quite a gash. I was living with my grandmother at the time in Long Beach. Miraculously [Ruffin] appeared on the scene just at that moment, staunched the bleeding, and carried me in his arms to a nearby clinic where the wound was stitched up. Whenever I look at the scar I inevitably think of my dear godfather. I visited with Ruffin at his home in upstate New York in the mid-1970s while on business in New York. I rented a plane and flew up to see him for several hours—a visit that turned out to be our last. He was my hero."

Young men were not "accepted" into the United States Naval Academy. They received an appointment, and that appointment was contingent on their excellent academic record, glowing personal references, and a stern medical exam. It was with great heartache that Minter was initially rejected. He failed the color perception exam and was marked down for "acne of back and chest with scarring." He had to wait ten nail-biting days in order to hear that, under re-examination, he had passed. Minter's dossier otherwise declared that he had a strong moral character. So perhaps it is not surprising that Minter should find among his Annapolis classmates many like-minded individuals who would become his closest and most loyal friends.

At seventeen years and four months old, Minter and the other appointees in his class reported to the Naval Academy in July 1928 to begin their "Plebe Summer." After dropping their gear in the designated area, they reported to take the oath of office as hundreds of men, in an unbroken line from the first class of 1845, had done before them. The officer administering the oath assured the young men assembled that it was one of the most important days of their lives.

Minter felt his throat go dry as he said the soul-stirring words: "I, Minter Dial, having been appointed a Midshipman in the United States Navy, do solemnly swear that I will support and defend the Constitution of the United States against all enemies foreign and domestic; that I will bear true faith and allegiance to the same; that I take this obligation freely, without any mental reservation or purpose of evasion; and that I will well and faithfully discharge the duties of the office on which I am about to enter, so help me God."

After taking the oath, Minter looked around the fabled Yard, as the campus was known.

Here, where the Severn River flowed into the Chesapeake Bay, were tree-shaded monuments that commemorated the bravery and heroism that has always been part of the Academy's heritage. The buildings and walkways on campus were named after graduates who had contributed both to naval history and the history of the county. Revolutionary War naval hero John Paul Jones was buried here. Under murderous enemy fire, Jones had yelled, "I have not yet begun to fight," and his words still served as a testament to the bravery that could be summoned up from the depths of a man's soul. Minter hoped if he ever went to war he could find the same within himself.

But first, he had to make it through the Academy.

All plebes were issued a handbook with a description of their course of study, hundreds of rules and regulations, and what was expected of each of them. Reading it, Minter was glad he had knuckled down and really studied while he was in school. There was a lot to learn, and he would have to keep his eye on the ball.[1]

Becoming a midshipman at the Academy wasn't like becoming a freshman at a regular college. You were expected to work harder than you'd ever worked before and to push yourself beyond your perceived limits in order to prepare for "the challenging responsibilities of service as a naval officer."[2]

Minter knew he was making a commitment to something larger than himself, and that thought made him feel proud, excited, and terrified.

He looked over the curriculum and found he'd be studying some humanities and social sciences; but the coursework would be heavy in engineering, science, and mathematics. Though it sounded tough, Minter was looking forward to challenging himself. If he was supposed to serve on a ship, it would be good to know something about them and how they ran. He didn't think the few times he had gone sailing with his cousins on Lake Rabon would cut it. He hadn't gone to Naval Prep School like some of the other guys (his father's Senate connections had spared him that), but he was eager to learn.

Yet the Academy wasn't just going to train his mind; his body would get a workout, too. This was what he had overheard from fellow prospective plebes swapping rumors on the train up from DC's Union Station.

"I hear you have to do a hundred fifty one-armed pushups a day in the first week or you wash out," one skinny kid had said.

"It's not the pushups I'm worried about," said the muscular guy sitting next to him. "It's that you have to run five miles in less than thirty minutes. Jeez, I'll drop dead if that's true."

Minter looked down at the small roll of fat around his waist and swallowed hard. He had always loved food, and ever since he left puberty, he found it all too easy to put on a few extra unwanted pounds. No more peanut-butter pie or fried chicken, he promised himself.

But now that he was finally here at the Academy, surrounded by buildings the very stones of which seemed to ring with history, Minter realized that the true lesson he would learn was about the importance of honor.

The Naval Academy had a stated mission: "To develop Midshipmen morally, mentally and physically and to imbue them with the highest ideals of duty, honor and loyalty, in order to graduate leaders who are dedicated to a career of naval service and have potential for future development in mind and character, to assume the highest responsibilities of command, citizenship and government. Our mission forms the basis for everything we do at the Academy. It also encourages a sense of spirit and pride.... "[3]

The officer in charge of their orientation said that, "The Academy [was] going to develop the Midshipmen to produce outstanding naval officers of competence, character and compassion; men privileged to lead sailors and Marines who have also volunteered to serve our country."

That development would start right now. Minter and the other plebes were told about the Honor Concept.

The Academy was run (as had been the British Navy from whence it took the code) on a concept of honor. Though this would later come to define the term "an officer and a gentleman," for now at Annapolis it demanded that midshipmen were persons of integrity. They would, to a man, embody the Honor Concept:

We stand for that which is right.

We tell the truth and ensure that the full truth is known. We do not lie.

We embrace fairness in all actions. We ensure that work submitted as our own is our own, and that assistance received from any source is authorized and properly documented. We do not cheat.

We respect the property of others and ensure that others are able to benefit from the use of their own property. We do not steal.[4]

Upright, honest, hardworking. These were concepts Minter understood, approved of, and, having been an Eagle Scout, already tried hard to practice.

Now he would try even harder.

DISMISSED BY THE officer, the men dispersed to head back to their dorm, Bancroft Hall, to get squared away. As he passed the Naval Academy Chapel, Minter, not an overly religious man despite his mother's best attempts to make him devout, threw a quick prayer heavenward.

"Here I go," he whispered. "Help me live up to this, please."

THE DORM AT Bancroft Hall housed the entire Brigade of Midshipmen. It contained 1,873 midshipmen rooms, nearly five miles of corridors, and about thirty-three acres of floor space, making it one of the largest single dormitories in the world. It's where Minter and his fellow midshipmen would study, sleep, and relax, but on that first day it was a scene of total chaos. There were guys everywhere, all studying handbooks and paperwork handed to them at orientation; looking for room numbers; juggling bags, bedding, and suitcases; and yelling instructions (or insults) down the halls at each other. The place already smelled like an old gym sock, thanks to hundreds of young men having just stood under the scorching sun of a Maryland summer day.

Minter elbowed his way through the melee and made it to his room just in time to meet his roommate, Charlie "Chuck" Keene.

Chuck and Minter had met at the very Western High School that had started my investigation. Chuck was a redheaded, rawboned bundle of energy, already hooked on his Navy career. He knew all the traditions and lore of the Academy well before even stepping foot inside. An inveterate lady's man, Chuck was known for his joyous disposition and for writing fanciful poems.

The two plebes shook hands, decided on which bed they'd take, and set to unpacking as they got reacquainted. They looked forward to fierce games of chess and backgammon and planned to become regular tennis partners. Chuck liked all manner of games, sleep, and girls, though not necessarily in that order. Minter smiled and heartily agreed, especially with the last item.

Minter's high school yearbook had taken note of his attraction for the fairer sex, which was so universally returned that the yearbook offered the suggestion that there be additional cars put on to Annapolis-bound trains to accommodate all the girls who would undoubtedly follow Minter to the Academy. Minter told Chuck he didn't have a girl at the moment, but he was keeping an eye out for one.

Chuck burst into song, "Five foot two, eyes of blue. But, oh, what those five feet could do. Has anybody seen my gal?" Laughing at himself, he said to Minter, "I just can't help it. I break out singing all the time. Guess I've got a song in my heart."

Minter laughed with him and was glad to be starting at Annapolis in such good company.

The two would become lifelong friends.

MINTER AND CHUCK became part of the Seventh Company, Fourth Battalion of the class of 1932. Minter also got to know and grow close to Frank Brumby (an admiral's son), Bob Leonard, Frank Wilder, and Corky Ward; but one fellow Southerner, who lived a few doors down in Bancroft Hall, would become a particular friend of Minter's—William Cox, aka "Ruffin."[5]

Bill "Ruffin" Cox was a tall man from North Carolina. Although his family's military legacy was in the army, Ruffin wanted to join the Navy because of the variety and travel. As Southerners, he and Minter bonded hard and fast. Ruffin was highly athletic and, with his long legs, was a fast runner. Minter and Ruffin often had long and passionate discussions about history and politics well into the night. You always knew where you stood with Ruffin.

While Minter enjoyed his friend's honesty and intelligence, Ruffin was considered by some of his fellow classmates to be a bit of a prig, highly religious, and a little too serious. Of Ruffin, the *Lucky Bag*, the Academy's yearbook, would write: "To call Bill an idle conversationalist would be blasphemy; for when he has something to say, it is usually worthwhile to listen. A square shooter and a good friend, he has every requirement for a good officer..."

The yearbook was correct. Cox would go on to become a rear admiral.

Minter gravitated to such high-minded friends and was high-minded himself. He was well-mannered, polished, and sought-after company at every party. He shone at cotillions, since he was an excellent dancer, a trait that made him popular with the ladies. It was this popularity that kept Minter, who never drank or smoked or failed to get high academic marks, from being perceived as a goody two-shoes. In fact, he was considered one of the "hot shots" of the company, and his friends found him so congenial, they gave Minter the nickname "Sun" in honor of his cheerful disposition.

Minter's friends also appreciated his considerable energy and competitive spirit, especially when put to good use on the lacrosse field. Among his teammates was George Washington Pressey from Hampton, Virginia. Square-chinned George, whose nickname was "Butch," was a quick-witted and fun-loving storyteller. George and Minter soon became firm friends and looked out for one another on and off the field. George was a man of his word. With broad shoulders and a voice that carried, George always made his presence known.

Lacrosse had started at the Academy in 1908, and the team had its first undefeated season by 1911. Though World War I had made the team cancel the season after only a couple of games, the Navy's lacrosse was undefeated from midseason 1916 to 1923, winning forty-five consecutive games. Minter donned his uniform, adorned with the blue and gold school colors first adopted in 1890, and joined his fellow "mids" on the field, including for his first Army-Navy game. When he heard the Navy band strike up "Anchors Aweigh" (a fight song written by the Academy's musical director in 1906), he felt a tingle go up his spine as he sang along:

> Stand Navy down the field,
> Sails set to the sky,
> We'll never change our course,
> So Army you steer shy.
> Roll up the score, Navy,
> Anchors Aweigh,
> Sail Navy down the field,
> And sink the Army,
> Sink the Army Grey.

Minter laughed out loud when he caught sight of Bill the Goat, the school mascot who had held pride of place (despite brief incursions by two dogs, a cat, and a carrier pigeon), since 1893, when officers of the USS *New York* donated him to help Navy triumph over Army, in the annual all-important Army-Navy game.

The goat wasn't the only mascot intended to bring luck to the team. The statue of Tecumseh, according to the handbook, had been an Annapolis resident since 1866. Originally the figurehead of the USS *Delaware*, it was meant to portray Tamanend, the great chief of the Delawares. It developed that Tamanend was a lover of peace and so did not strike the fancy of the Brigade. Looking for another name, midshipmen referred to the figurehead as "Powhatan" and "King Philip" before finally settling on Tecumseh, the fierce Shawnee chieftain who lived from 1768 to 1813. The original wooden statue was replaced after some fifty years in the open weather by a durable bronze replica, presented by the Class of 1891. Before the Army-Navy competition in any sport, Tecumseh got a fresh coat of war paint. He also got a lot of left-handed salutes and a shower of pennies—offerings for victory.

Minter proved to be a valuable addition to the team, never warming the bench, as most first-year players would find themselves doing. Years later, Minter's classmate Tom Nisewaner would recall, "We had the good fortune to play lacrosse together for our four years as midshipmen. We both played first string as plebes on the team . . . . You form a delightful bond when you play together that long in a rugged sport like lacrosse. You share a lot of things together and begin a friendship that lasts."

Starting in 1926, the United States Intercollegiate Lacrosse Association (USILA) began rating college lacrosse teams and awarding gold medals to the top teams. Navy shared the National Championship title in 1928 after it received the gold medal alongside Johns Hopkins, the University of Maryland, and Rutgers—each of which had only one regular-season collegiate defeat. In 1929, Navy was recognized again when it and Union College were both presented with gold medals. Minter joined the team in 1929 and his lacrosse team was a national champion that year. He was a proud member of the varsity team until his graduation.[6]

Minter had the thrilling experience of hearing the Gokokuji Bell (the replica of the 1456 casting brought to this country by Cmdre. Matthew C. Perry following his expedition to Japan in 1854), rung in front of Bancroft Hall.[7] The bell was only rung whenever the Army team was defeated. Minter was also very proud to earn the "N-Star," given only to those varsity athletes who had participated in those victories.

But, even more important than winning, Minter was finally part of the tradition of the Navy team facing the stands, putting their hands over their hearts, and singing "The Blue and Gold":

Now, colleges from sea to sea
May sing of colors true;
But who has better right than we
To hoist a symbol hue?
For sailors brave in battle fair,
Since fighting days of old,
Have proved the sailor's right to wear
The Navy Blue and Gold.

During his time at the Academy, Minter did indeed learn about those ships about which he was curious. Reinforcing the training he got in the classroom, every summer was devoted to "fleet alignment." For four weeks, the midshipmen were immersed in the fleet. The Third Class Summer saw them as part of the crew of a surface ship, taking part in the operations and drills and serving underway watches. The Second Class Summer had them complete their professional training as midshipmen and introduced them to the missions and equipment of the major Navy branches and those of the Marine Corps. They flew in Navy aircraft, dove in submarines, participated in Marine Corps combat training, and steered Navy ships. In their First Class Summer, the men acted as division officers in training, interacting with a wardroom and chief petty officer. They chose cruise options like surface, submarines, aviation, ordnance disposal, and Marine Corps training, to help them decide on their preferences prior to receiving their service assignment during their final fall semester.[8]

Minter's years at Annapolis passed quickly. Every morning, he rose at 5:30 and saluted to "Taps," a song handed down from Union Army Gen. Daniel Butterfield, with time to fit in a few pushups and jumping jacks; answered an all-hands Reveille at 6:30 a.m.; formed up for the morning meal at 7:00 a.m., and was in class from 7:55 a.m. to 3:30 p.m., with only a brief period for noon meal formation. He squeezed in lacrosse between 3:35 and

6:00 p.m., grabbed an evening meal at 6:30 p.m., studied from 8:00 to 11:00 p.m., and closed his books when "Taps" played "lights out" at midnight for all midshipmen.

If routine and schedules dominated his weekly life, Minter's passage at Annapolis was not without incident. Aside from two separate trips to the campus hospital, he also suffered an accident in his first year that could have been much more severe. In January 1929, Minter fired a pistol with a defective cartridge that narrowly missed his eye. Bandaged up, he notched it up as yet another "war" story.

On the weekends, meanwhile, Minter and some of the young men would borrow a car and head into the nation's capital, ostensibly to go to the Smithsonian or to visit Minter's or Chuck's family. Their main objective, however, was to meet girls. They walked from the Capitol to the Washington Monument and back again as they told each other about what they'd do when they found the "girl of their dreams" and bragged about their (largely invented) experiences with them. They punched each other's shoulders, laughed at the stupidest things, swore they'd be friends forever, and wondered aloud where they'd be stationed. They were generally even more innocent than they appeared, intrinsically braver than they believed, and so very young. They had seen each other through some scrapes, worried about each other's grades, cheered for each other at games, counseled each other through fears of the future, and talked about what concepts such as honor really meant. They had raised their bar of conduct and formed a true *esprit de corps*. They had become, without even realizing it, a band of brothers.

Through it all, Minter applied himself to his studies with great single-mindedness—until he became most thoroughly distracted by a young woman he dubbed "the Ultimate." About this time, in the middle of his third year, despite playing on the lacrosse team, he did get an official warning for "deficiencies in physical training." Presumably he doubled down on his effort and made up for the apparent lapses. But he was faced with the classic, if not ultimate, temptation.

This paragon of feminine virtue stopped Minter in his tracks, and he proposed almost immediately. She was Louise Brooks, the beautiful and well-bred daughter of a Philadelphia Main Line family. The two were expected to be married immediately after graduation, and Minter could speak of little else to his classmates.

But Louise's grandmother, the matriarch of the family, had different ideas. Though from a family of Southern aristocracy, Minter's lineage was not considered to be of blue enough blood (or Yankee enough inclination) for Louise's family, and she was strongly encouraged to marry another.

Minter was not the only one to be heartbroken at this turn of events. His classmate, Henry Hull, later opined that Louise never got over Minter.

"She married whom the grandmother wanted her to, and they were divorced within the year," Hull said. "She then married again, but that also led to divorce. I don't think she ever stopped loving Minter."

Time, though, really did heal all wounds, and Minter's heart mended as he and his classmates crammed for the all-important final exams. The day the grades were published, Minter and Hull, finding themselves delayed because of a visit to Minter's family in DC, broke every traffic law and terrified fellow motorists as they raced back to the Academy to see how they'd performed.

They'd done just fine.

EVEN BEFORE HE opened his eyes, Minter ran his thumb over his finger and the heavy metal band encasing it. He felt the class crest and the winged horse with a rider blowing a shell and carrying a trident. As long as he lived, he knew he'd be proud to wear his class ring, proud to be a member of the Naval Academy Class of 1932. He'd worked hard, sweating his way around the track to keep his weight down and make the demanding physical requirements; doing as he was told by officers and upperclassmen who hazed plebes until they were upperclassmen themselves; staying up all night studying for that trigonometry exam that he dreaded like no other. He was always worrying, working, wondering what the future held and finally, finally—today was the day. Minter smiled to himself as he swung his legs out of his bunk and his feet hit the familiar floor of Bancroft Hall. It was June 2, 1932. Graduation Day.

Commissioning Week had been a hell of a week already. It started with the Seamanship and Navigation Awards (Minter won a ribbon) and the Class of 1932 Ring Dance, where he made use of his best dance moves, and his easy smile made quite an impression on the females present. Then came the band, brass, and ensemble concerts; the "N" Reception for designated midshipmen, of which Minter was one; the Superintendent's Reception; silent drill platoon's performance and decidedly noisier pipe and drums performance; glee club and gospel choir shows; baccalaureate church services; the graduation ball; color parades to honor the winners of the year-long color competition where the thirty companies accumulated points for academic, professional, and intramural excellence; the dean's awards; and photo sessions by the dozen. It was noisy, exhausting, exhilarating, and a lot of fun. All of Minter's friends acted like grade-school kids on vacation, with pranks and jokes and towel-snapping being the order of the day, alongside promises to stay in touch and the sharing of wild rumors and speculation about their upcoming assignments.

Finally, the soon-to-be graduates made their way to Dahlgren Hall, where they sat trying not to be too boisterous, despite their excitement, as Secretary of the Navy Charles Francis Adams addressed them:

> "It is a real pleasure to represent our government this morning and to bring to you the warm regards of your countrymen. Few hearts fail to beat a little faster when they see your fine regiment

and know you are dedicating your lives to your country. I want you to feel that in that devotion you are serving ... kindly warm-hearted men and women who respect you ...

"It cannot, however, be fairly said, that you are making a sacrifice in joining the Navy.

There are few lives more satisfactory than that of an officer. You are to have all the mechanical interest of your ship, its care, its use and development. You have the interest of your men, their safety, their well-being, and their training. You will have the real joy of handling your ship when the time comes for that ...

"From the dawn of time, life on this earth has been a struggle; survival of the fittest, competition in which the strongest ... animal, the strongest man or country has won in war or commerce, and, by that winning, survived. Civilization has modified that rule of nature; but even now, the rules of fierce competition for success do not eliminate all that is unjust or without honor.... Laws cannot eliminate chance, favor, advantages of birth and riches, a thousand things that bring bitterness, even despair, to those without them. Out there are joy and despair, success and failure, that strange mixture of good and bad that marks civilization, but always a fierce struggle with few rules and much that is just luck.

"What conditions do we offer? Not perfection surely, but we know we must work in harmony or someday die. We all know that men are the greater element of native strength than the ships they control. We all know that navies, limited and balanced in strength as they are, that the Navy will win the next war that has the best organization [sic]. Individuals ordering blind obedience will not often win. Victory will go to that combination of men that has developed the greatest unity of action; the best spirit. That spirit is a strange, fleeting thing hard to define, harder to secure. Those who can secure it have the great quality of leadership. They will rise highest. The Navy with the greatest number of those men who can also think will win wars.

"I'll not try to tell you how to lead, even if I knew. It would be like lecturing to you on the attributes of character, on the things men love, on the principles of justice ... I only venture to suggest that you study the art. Begin, if you will, with friendship. Start with the spirit of your class. Cherish it, improve it with each year. Spread your good spirit through this service of ours ... contribute the next element of success in organization—justice.

"We crave your happiness.... To have it you must succeed. To be sure, you cannot all be first, but success as a basis of happiness is relative. Success that means that you must accomplish what your brains entitle you to, so that when your career is ending you may not have the bitterness of regret. You must know you have done your best. How will you accomplish that? ...

"Life, happiness is for you to make. You can drift, enjoy life for a time, and someday land on the beach.... It takes real courage to plot your course and stick to it hard 'til success comes; but by that course, only happiness is sure. You will go through that way if you have in your souls the real courage of fighting men you pretend to be."[9]

Minter sat with his classmates and listened to the speakers, the dean, and other notables tell the young men present what an honor it was to join the ranks of those heroes who had gone before them into the Navy's illustrious ranks. He felt a swelling in his chest, tempered only by the fear that he might not prove worthy of the honor. He made a silent vow to himself just then that he would pledge his honor and his very life if need be in service to his country. He would live up to the fact that soon he would be a graduate of the greatest military academy of all of them—the United States Naval Academy. He felt the weight of that responsibility as surely as he felt the weight of the heavy gold of his class ring resting on his finger.

Secretary Adams then presented the graduates with their hard-earned sheepskins. Minter rose when he heard his name called and walked forward to get his diploma, feeling very proud when he heard, "N. Minter Dial has attained the rank of ensign."

When everyone had gotten their sheepskins, the graduation ceremony was finally over, and the graduates followed a long and hallowed tradition: they took their hats off and threw their covers high in the air. A mighty cheer rose from their throats. They had graduated!

He found himself surrounded by his classmates. Minter gave a bear hug to George Pressey, his pal from the lacrosse team; punched the arms of David McDougal, Bill Bull, and Harry Hull; and suffered a damn near painful scrum from Tom Nisewaner, his fellow lacrosse first-stringer. He gave a face-splitting grin to Chuck Keene, with whom he had shared so many ferocious tennis and chess battles and with whom he hoped to soon share orders for a West Coast cruise. When the crowd finally parted, Minter saw his family standing nearby.

Striding over, Minter submitted to the fierce hugs of his aunts, his two lovely sisters, and the younger Joseph, and then a gentler hug from his mother, whom he saw was crying. He noticed the glint of tears in his father's eyes as the senator took his hand and told him how very proud his son had made him. Minter knew in that moment that it had all been worth it.

When Minter excused himself to go change out of his dress uniform, he pushed his way past the rest of his classmates, all of whom were surrounded by equally proud family members. He made his way past Tecumseh, decked out for graduation day in war paint and feathers, gave the old Indian a quick salute, and stood for a moment in the only quiet spot he could find in the yard. At over six feet tall, perfectly muscled after his years of physical training and in fine health, Minter was the picture of a handsome, healthy young man with the whole world before him. A sunbeam hit his face, leaving no shadow behind, as he stepped into his future.

None of them knew that war clouds were gathering.[10]

— 4 —

O NE OF THE most remarkable and moving parts of researching Minter's story has been the discovery of the incredible
love between my grandparents. Reading their passionate,
emotionally open correspondence brought their story vividly to
life for me. It was easy for me to imagine them together, dancing,
laughing, and falling quickly in love. At times, I felt like I was reading a diary, and surely these letters were not intended for others
to read. Uncovering their deep love was at once charming as well
as unsettling as a backdrop for the events that were to unfold. It
was, as I learned, a magnificent love affair.

And yet, on paper, Lisa Porter seemed an unlikely match for
Minter. While many girls her age would have been content to
spend their time dreaming of a handsome young officer in a smart
uniform, Lisa had bigger dreams. She planned a glamorous career,
her name in lights, and, of course, an Academy Award statue
inscribed with her name: *Elisabeth W. Porter, Best Actress, 1932.*

Lisa wasn't alone in her dreams, of course. The entire town of
Hollywood was chock-full of gorgeous young girls from all over
the country who hoped to catch the eye of a casting director and
hit it big in the movies. They arrived on trains and buses by the
handful—from Iowa and Indiana and Illinois—with everything

they owned in one suitcase and enough money to last a week or two before disaster struck.

Lisa didn't have that problem. Her mother, Grace Burgdorf Porter, had barely missed a beat when, soon after giving birth to a daughter in 1909, she separated from her husband, William Porter. Grace was the daughter of a Methodist minister based in southern Michigan. She became a teacher and was voted "prettiest school marm" by a wide margin, receiving a silk parasol as her prize. She had moved to New York with her mother in 1903, and, in 1908, married William, the son of a wealthy timber baron. However, she seemed to have fallen for a man with less than sterling character. The marriage was short-lived but lasted long enough to produce Elisabeth. In 1914, Grace turned her house into a private school: Mrs. Porter's School for Girls, which Lisa attended. Grace polished her plans to make her daughter a star.[1]

Meanwhile, Porter died of drink in 1917, leaving his widow and young daughter enough money to lead a comfortable life including a large house on the Pacific Ocean in Long Beach, California, trips to Europe, and annual vacations in Hawaii.

Grace had been a somewhat celebrated amateur actress— albeit locally—in her youth, and a bit of that stardust rubbed off on Lisa, who would sit for hours peppering her mother with questions about her theatrical adventures. The pair pored over industry magazines like *Silver Screen,* which offered articles telling girls how to perfect their curves as Joan Crawford did; *Photoplay*, for advice on how to achieve glamour like Carole Lombard; and *Movie Classics*, depicting the fairytale life and romance of Hollywood royalty Mary Pickford and Douglas Fairbanks, who ascended to their estate, Pickfair, as the gods had once repaired to Olympus.

Lisa ate up every word.

She plucked her eyebrows to the thinnest of lines, tried every new variety of face powder, bobbed her hair, did sit-ups daily with a ten-pound salt bag on her stomach, and learned every new dance to perfection. She also went to the movies several times a week, sometimes arriving for a matinee and sitting through so many showings that it was dark when she left the theater. She could recite lines from her favorites—*Shanghai Express*, with Marlene Dietrich playing Shanghai Lily, or *Red Dust*, in which Jean Harlow and Clark Gable sizzled on the screen. She laughed out loud at the Marx Brothers in *Duck Soup* and felt a small thrill at being attracted to the bad guys, Paul Muni and George Raft, in *Scarface*.

Lisa was young but knew a few things about herself: She was a pretty girl—maybe not show-stopping like Harlow (Lisa had briefly considered bleaching her brown hair to a lustrous platinum), but a pretty girl, nonetheless. She was tall, slender, and had the long legs necessary to show off the seamed silk stockings she favored.

Lisa also knew that personality could make even a plain face beautiful (look at Bette Davis), and she practiced what her mother always told her—"Let your smile reach your eyes, Lisa." She smiled a lot and particularly at men, but not enough to be considered a tease, like her friend Helen Goodloe. Helen was what she had heard a man call a "round heels"—the type of girl it didn't take much to push on to her back because of her loose morals. Lisa knew better than that. "Why buy the bakery when you can have all the bread for free?" her mother used to say, and Lisa agreed. She would be saving herself for marriage, though she was sure that was many years off. For now, Lisa was just flirting, and it was all harmless fun.

She also knew she was a good actress and singer. All through school, she had jumped at the chance to perform onstage. Musicals, class plays, ensemble shows—she even volunteered to do some scenes and sing some songs at local old folks' homes. She liked an audience, and the audience always seemed to like her.

She read the pages of *Variety* voraciously and went to open auditions, or "cattle calls." She had even been awarded a few parts as an extra in a crowd scene for a couple of the studios, but she had yet to make her big-screen debut. She was willing to wait, though not too patiently.

While not a stage mother, Grace was entirely supportive of her daughter's dreams to make it big in Hollywood and always made sure Lisa was front and center in all performances given at Mrs. Porter's School. She made use of every avenue to have Lisa seen by all the right people.

Her mother believed that connections were the ticket to her daughter's well-deserved fame and cultivated all she could gather through her school's Rolodex. She also made use of a very good family connection. Her sister's husband, with a name straight out of *The Mask of Zorro*, Don Francisco, was an influential bicoastal banker and real-estate impresario. He knew everyone who was anyone in the film colony and gave lavish parties at his mansion. Grace made sure she and Lisa were invited to them all.

Lisa was an intriguing figure and was the subject of many proposals. On one celebrated trip, Lisa—age twenty-two—was invited to join Baron Jean Empain on his huge world-circling yacht, the *Heliopolis,* for a private cruise to Hawaii. Grace imposed one condition: that she be invited as a chaperone. So Grace came along. No romance came out of this trip.

At another party, however, Lisa's destiny walked right through the door.

AFTER GRADUATION AND his commission as ensign, Minter was given his first orders: he was to report to the battleship USS *Arizona,* berthed in San Pedro, California.

The *Arizona,* named in honor of the forty-eighth state's admission to the union, was the last of the Pennsylvania class of super-dreadnought battleships and one of the ships which accompanied President Wilson as he attended the Paris Peace Conference at the end of World War I.

With an overall length of 608 feet, a beam of 97 feet, and a draft of 29 feet 3 inches at deep load, this was 25 feet longer than the older ships. She carried twelve 14-inch, 45-caliber guns in triple-gun turrets and one hundred shells for each gun. The ship mounted four 3-inch, 50-caliber guns for anti-aircraft defense and also mounted two 21-inch torpedo tubes, carrying twenty-four torpedoes. Most importantly, she carried a highly skilled crew of fifteen hundred, including fifty officers.[2]

She was, as the *New York Times* declared at her commissioning, "The world's biggest and most powerful, both offensively and defensively, super dreadnought ever constructed."[3]

Minter felt a great sense of pride when he reported to the massive ship. The USS *Arizona* was the embodiment of the strength and might of the United States, and Minter was both awed and humbled that he was getting to join the crew of such a majestic vessel.

Since the country was not at war, the *Arizona* was mostly used for training exercises, like the one in which she participated in February of 1932—Grand Joint Exercise No. 4, in which carrier aircraft successfully attacked Pearl Harbor in a haunting precursor to the actual events that would take place in December of 1941. But the *Arizona* also helped out with a real crisis: in 1933, an earthquake struck nearby Long Beach, and Minter and the rest of the crew helped evacuate victims.

Minter's shipmate for his first two years on the *Arizona* was his friend, Ruffin Cox, who was witness to Minter's cutting a small swath through the starlets or would-be starlets found everywhere. In an effort to recover from his broken heart over Louise, Minter wasted no time in procuring a ramshackle old car and using it to burn up the miles between San Pedro and Hollywood. Ruffin proved helpful in this endeavor, as he had a family connection of his own: Cecil B. DeMille, the legendary film director—whose *Ten Commandments* had proven to be one of the most successful films of the silent era—was Ruffin's cousin. It was DeMille who invited Ruffin and Minter to a party at his palatial home.

Ruffin and Minter arrived in their dress whites, each looking like every girl's dream of a military man. With his erect bearing, dark hair and eyes, and undeniable charm, Minter caused quite a stir in the room by his very presence. He was aware of the attention and enjoyed it, noticing the pretty girls in the room, but he wasn't yet over the heartbreak handed to him by Louise. Minter was determined to date lots of girls and keep things casual with them all.

That plan went right out the window shortly thereafter.

Minter's shipmate and good friend, Chuck Keene, also enjoyed the Los Angeles lifestyle and its abundance of beautiful young women. One memorable night, Minter and Chuck stopped by the grill of the Pacific Coast Club, a huge wedding cake of a building erected in 1926, featuring turrets and towers, wood-paneled libraries, a gentlemen's boxing ring, a view of the ocean that was truly stunning, and a legendary bar frequented by film stars and showgirls. The crowd around the piano was thick, and several couples had taken to the large dance floor when Minter and Chuck walked in.

They ordered drinks, and Minter was about to rib Chuck about ordering a martini just to look sophisticated when Chuck said, "Oh, look, it's Lisa. I know that girl." Enjoying the party scene as he did, Chuck knew a lot of girls. Turning toward where Chuck was pointing, Minter's eyes caught Lisa's, and time seemed to stop. The noise of the bar faded away, and Minter realized he was holding his breath. He exhaled, slid off his stool, and strode directly over to the circle of people surrounding Lisa. The crowd parted for him as though making way for him to assume his natural place by her side. Minter sharply elbowed Chuck for an introduction, and as he took Lisa's hand, he knew two things: he had never seen a girl so lovely and he was looking at his future wife.

BEING PRETTY AND vivacious guaranteed Lisa plenty of suitors buzzing around her, jockeying for a chance to date the girl with the laughing eyes. She was no wallflower and went out with many of them; but though she certainly intended someday to earn her "MRS Degree," she was in no hurry. Plenty of time to tie herself down after she had established her acting career.

That timeline was hastily rewritten when she met Minter Dial.

As he took her hand and slightly bowed over it while telling her how enchanted he was to meet her in an accent redolent of magnolias and moonlight, Lisa felt her pulse trip a little. She knew she shouldn't be bowled over by a man in a uniform—so cliché—yet he was undeniably handsome and thoroughly charming, and Lisa felt her resolution slip away.

The two danced the night away, far surpassing anyone else on the dance floor, coming together as though they had been partners for decades instead of minutes, dancing as though they were meant for each other.

In between sets, they shared a leather banquette in a quiet corner and talked about life and their dreams of the future. Minter wanted a family. Lisa did too, but she wanted a chance to pursue her acting career first. Minter agreed she should do whatever made her happy. He wanted his wife to be fulfilled. At the mention of the word "wife," Lisa felt a flush rise to her cheeks, and she knew he was talking about her.

She would go to sleep that night practicing the sound of the name "Mrs. Lisa Dial" and finding it didn't sound half bad.

LISA AND MINTER dated as often as he could get leave over the next few months, and not three months had passed when he made the decision to ask Lisa to marry him. He reached this conclusion after pacing the deck of the ship for hours and finally descending at 3:00 a.m. to rouse Ruffin to tell him of his decision.

Ruffin thought it was his duty, as friend and fellow Southerner, to demand that Minter slow down and observe a proper period of courting as he would have done back home in South Carolina. Ruffin raked him over the coals, but his real intention was to persuade Minter that Lisa and her family were not "their sort." Ruffin's natural priggishness was showing through again as he told Minter that Lisa had dated lots of men, had no real family background, and seemed to have tawdry show-business dreams: she was too much of a "high-stepper" for Minter.

Amused, Minter thanked Ruffin for his concern and entirely ignored his advice. He was going to propose to Lisa as soon as possible before some other guy snapped her up.

Minter and Lisa were married four months later, on March 24, 1934.

Don Francisco insisted on having the wedding and reception at his residence, an old Monterey Colonial–style house, in Pasadena, California. Minter asked Charlie Keene to be his best man, and, in spite of his friend's initial objection to the match, invented a new role, head usher, for Ruffin Cox. In addition to Ruffin, there were five other ushers, only one of whom came from the north: Ens. Malcolm Douglas of Vermont, who would be with Minter later on in the war. Also in attendance were many friends from Annapolis, including classmate George Pressey, whose wife Betty Lee was one of Lisa's bridesmaids. Lisa, for her part, was one of the most beautiful brides ever to walk down the aisle. And while Minter's family members were unable to attend the wedding, his parents would no doubt have seen a glimmer of their influence in a write-up of the event in the *Washington Post*, which noted, "Dancing will be a feature of the evening."

AFTER A HONEYMOON during which the couple drove cross-country to Washington, DC, to visit Minter's family, Minter was ordered to join the crew of the USS *Gilmer*, a Clemson-class destroyer, for more training exercises. Soon after, he was transferred to the USS *Brooks*, another Clemson-class destroyer assigned to the Scouting Force.

In June of 1935, Minter was promoted to lieutenant (junior grade) and began a tour of duty that included stints in Seattle, Buffalo, and Newport. During Minter's prolonged absences, he and Lisa would write to one another long, intimate, and florid love letters. Fortunately, there were also prolonged leaves, and it was back in Long Beach that Lisa gave birth to the couple's first child, Victor, on June 21, 1938.

Minter's duties allowed him lots of time on shore, as he had been assigned to the repair ship, the USS *Medusa,* and had nine months to get to know his first-born son. With a regular schedule on the *Medusa,* always a rarity in the Navy, Minter and Lisa found time to host dinner parties for shipmates like Ruffin Cox, George Pressey, and Chuck Keene.

A sailor's pay being what it is, no one had much money, but everyone would chip in a dollar or two. Lisa would throw together whatever ingredients she had on hand for dinner, and they'd pass the evening reading to each other. Lisa was able to put her acting talents to use, and she ended up acting out most of the scenes from the night's chosen book.

She also put another talent to work at those parties. She whipped up pitchers of daiquiris, very welcome by the guests but less welcome by Minter, who didn't drink. Lisa drank enough for the both of them, and, rather than argue with her, Minter eventually gave in and would grudgingly have a daiquiri. He tried not to notice she drank more than he did. After all, he reasoned, she deserved to relax and enjoy herself. She was, in his eyes, a wonderful wife and the perfect mother. He knew he was a lucky man.

Lisa doted on Minter. She was always fretting about his looks and ensuring that his uniform was impeccable. Lisa even took to reminding him of things he sometimes forgot, becoming his to-do list in human form. After Minter once ran out of gas when driving back from an assignment, Lisa would always remind him to check the gas gauge. She made sure he always had a pressed handkerchief. She closed the top button on his raincoat on blustery days. She couldn't get close enough to him. His strong personality complemented her anxiousness, and it was as though she tried to make literal the wedding vow "and the two shall become one."

Minter was eventually given a land-based assignment back in Annapolis with the Bureau of Navigation as an instructor of English. Once there, his friend from high school and former lacrosse teammate, now-Capt. William Bull, told Minter that volunteers were being requested to go to the Philippines, which had been granted independence by President Franklin Roosevelt on the very same day Minter and Lisa were married. Now the Navy was asking Annapolis graduates to serve as a police force to circumvent escalating tensions between factions in that country. According to Bull, Minter even tested his wife's reaction by claiming to have volunteered for duty in the Philippines, but when she howled with protest was quick to reassure her that he was only kidding. After all, reasoned Minter, there was no need to put himself in harm's way. It wasn't like there was a war on.

On September 1, 1939, Germany invaded Poland.

IN APRIL 1940, the Dials greeted their daughter, Diana, and, in December, said farewell to Minter's father, who died at the age of seventy-eight. These were only two of many hellos and goodbyes soon to come.

The drums of war beat on, with Germany invading the Netherlands, Belgium, and France and making plans to invade Russia. The Battle of Britain lit the skies over the English countryside in the summer and fall of 1940, and the RAF fought gallantly. Japan and China were fighting in the East, with Japan capturing cities in Northern China, Hankou in Central China, and Guangzhou in the South. In May, Belgium capitulated, and in June, France signed an armistice with Germany. Mainland Europe was now under German occupation with the forces of the Reich ruling the sea and air. In September, Italy, Germany, and Japan joined together in the Rome-Berlin-Tokyo Axis.

That same month, the Luftwaffe began bombing London in the nightmare known as the Blitz. As Londoners crawled into tunnels, Churchill called President Roosevelt from his underground bunker, insisting that the US join the war. For the following year, the US military and the War Department prepared for war without express approval or need.[4]

Back in Annapolis, the Dials and their circle of friends, mostly classmates of Minter's from the Academy and couples with young children, ate, drank, and made merry at parties that rotated from house to house. Those attending tried to ignore the ominous signs that the men at the events might soon be called up should America enter the war. The laughter became louder, the booze flowed more freely, and the gags got sillier. "Whistling past the graveyard" would be a good description of that time. The wives hoped against hope that their men wouldn't be taken away.

— 5 —

They that go down to the sea in ships, that do business in great waters;
These see the works of the Lord, and his wonders in the deep.

PSALM 107:23

I N JULY 1941, Minter was ordered to sea. Ever the responsible one, before heading off, he wrote a letter to his extended family, not only detailing all he had done to put his late father's estate in order, but telling them how he could be reached and asking them to write:

> Dear Family,
> ... I sail 8 August for Cavite, P.I., on the President Garfield. After that my address will be U.S. Asiatic Fleet, c/o P.M., San Francisco, California. Please write to me often. I shall be thinking of you all. Best of luck.
> Fondly,
> Minter[1]

Then he spent a last night with his wife and children. It was a night fraught with emotion and one he recalled in a letter home later:

My very dearest wife,

Three months ago tonight we were together for our last night of living before this long separation. We experienced all emotions that night—joy, sorrow, peace and turmoil, ecstasy and contentment.... I know that when we are together again, it will seem that we have never been apart. That is the wonderful thing about married love—it is so permanent. Ours will last for always. I love you darling.

Minter

The *President Garfield* was a large and grandly appointed passenger ship, carrying both civilians and soldiers to Manila via Honolulu, Shanghai, and Hong Kong. The Navy men on board awaited further orders en route to Manila; but for the beginning part of the passage, they had little to do except eat, sleep, play deck sports, write letters, and miss their loved ones.

Minter's first cable was one of the dozens of telegrams sent to wives and loved ones at home from departing servicemen, which displayed a chin-up attitude and reflected none of the fear of sailing into the unknown the men must have felt:

WESTERN UNION

SAILING AT THREE. KEEP THE HOME FIRES BURNING.

ALL MY LOVE.

MINTER

In all Minter's letters home during this period, the tone of the correspondence was upbeat, almost relentlessly cheerful, and kept his wife engaged in his daily activities, as he asked her to do with hers and the children's (young Victor, now three, whom he called often "Butch" or "Sailor," and Diana, just fifteen months old):

Because I love you more than words can tell and am counting on you to take the place of Daddy and Mother until I get back. You must be happy to keep Butch and Diana happy!

... [About] Vic's school, and the birthday party... it makes me so proud to hear that he is doing well and is "manly!" He started out that way and I believe he will always be so. I was amazed to hear that he sang; if he carried a tune that proves he is like you in at least that!

. . .

Can't wait to see the snap shots, movies (in spite of your pessimism), record, etc. You might kinda, sorta take another reel and not wait so long again, maybe! Gosh but I love you, and am proud of you and our family.

. . .

Goodnight darling. Hug the children for me and tell Vic that I'm trying very hard to be brave because I must be away! It is harder than you will ever know.

Yours for always,
Minter

. . .

Sweetheart darling... I have so much to be thankful for. I have you and our children. We have our love, our health and our happiness. I like the word "our." It signifies "sharing" and joint possession. Things seem so much more important when they are shared with one we love. We share "everything" from memories to belongings. I adore you, you are precious....

. . .

... [It is] wonderful to have you and the children to love, to think about and to plan for, you give my life a stability and are my reason for being. Everything I do is for "us." I love you darling. Don't ever forget that.

Yours for always,
Minter

. . .

... I like to have you tell me the things you think and feel as well as all the details of what you do. Sometimes, for hours at night, I think and live over wonderful times we have had together, the thrills and joys we have known and shared. At times, it is almost more than I can stand, but manage somehow to look to the future and realize that we will be together and that then it will seem that we have never been apart.

. . .

The description of Diana hugging you and patting your back made me long for some of the same. She is so gentle and Victor such a boy. [In your last letter,] the sketch of "our life together" was written so much like a storybook maybe you should write it as such! It brought tears of happiness to my eyes. It is tons reassuring and comforting in these days of separation to have a really beautiful love. Ours is 100% perfect with our family and all.

. . .

Goodnight darling—Remember about me loving you. You make me awful proud by carrying on and keeping the home a "real" home for our children. When people ask me if I'm married—I say very much so and have a son and a daughter! That means even more than saying "two" children! Hug them for me. I long to smother you with kisses and will again soon because even two years aren't long when we have a lifetime ahead!

Yours for always,

Minter

By mid-August, Minter admitted in a letter to Lisa that he expected to receive his orders in the next few days and that he was "curious." When the ship crossed the 180th meridian with still no word received, Minter and his fellow officers got together for a cocktail party (at which Minter was bartender) to reassure each other that they weren't worried. After a night of toasting and boasting, Minter confessed to such a hangover from imbibing the "Dutch Courage," "no one could even sell him a drink of any kind."

One week later, the men got their first look at Shanghai, and Minter realized just how far he was from the clean and sunny shores of the US.

... Have just gotten back aboard after seeing all I ever want to
see of Shanghai! It is hard to believe that people could live in
such filth and squalor. They say you become accustomed to seeing it and then it doesn't bother you. But I am afraid it will take
me a long time to become accustomed to it.

The sights so upset him, he didn't even feel able to write Lisa
his daily long letter:

Didn't write much last night as was too depressed by what I had
seen. Feeling better today; at least the sea air is clean...

Manila presented a better vista. The *Garfield* docked in Manila
Harbor on Pier 7 on September 6.

Situated on the western coast of the Philippines, Manila was a
busy port, and, thanks to the American occupation of 1899, was
a thriving city. Filled with expats, officers, and enlisted men of all
the US military branches, their wives, families, and servants, as
well as the largest population of Filipinos, Manila afforded rec-
reational opportunities, shops, entertainment venues (including
dozens of nightclubs), and the home away from home for officers,
the Army Navy Club.

Minter made great use of that venue (chits were signed for
daily use, making it easy to forget that a bill would be presented
monthly for payment, Minter bemoaned in a letter to Lisa), as well
as meeting fellow officers for golf games, horseback riding, movies, dinners at local French and Japanese restaurants, and regular
rounds of tennis. He found the court at Olongapo Bay the perfect
venue to blow off steam and channel his competitive nature. The
games also gave him a goal to shoot for in what was increasingly
an atmosphere fraught with frustration at what appeared to be a
waste of his Academy training. His determination to make something of himself in the USN appeared stymied by the enforced life
of leisure.

But soon his days would no longer be spent on just "getting a great tan" and trying to keep his weight down after eating all the "good food." In what must have been a moment of great personal pride, Minter was given his first command—the USS *Napa*, a Bagaduce-class tugboat, commissioned first in WWI and decommissioned in 1929 (joining the inactive fleet berthed at Olongapo in the Philippines). As war in Asia loomed closer, the *Napa* was recommissioned to join the US Navy's Asiatic Fleet. Minter rushed to tell Lisa the news.

> 11 September, 1941
> Sweetheart darling,
>   ... So much has happened that I don't know where to start! First of all I am to be the commanding officer of the Napa.... I am delighted with the job, couldn't possibly have anything better.
>   Tom Warfield got the Bittern, which is a little better ship, but he is senior to me.... The Flag Sec for CINCAF (Cinc Asiatic Fleet) met us with our orders....

Minter was thrilled to be given a command, even if his ship was an old coal-burner fitted with WWI technology. The *Napa* was sturdy, ocean-going, and, as crewmember Machinist's Mate 2nd Class H. L. Richardson said, "The Napa had a helluva reputation."

For his part, Minter, now the "Skipper" or "Old Man," had to build a reputation with his crew.

"We heard he was the son of famous Senator Dial from South Carolina. Also, that he was coming from a duty in Washington. This sort of disturbed us because it gave the thought of a 'spit-and-polish Navy,' which the *Napa* definitely was not, due to the job that the ship was made for as a combatant ship. We did *not* adhere to a spit-and-polish routine. When Lieutenant Dial came aboard and assumed command, we were pleased that he did not show that he was going to be a spit-and-polish officer,"

recalled William Wells, chief gunner's mate and chief petty officer. "Apparently the previous commander had told him about
the ship. Captain Dial seemed to fit in with the ship, the job, and
the men. It was obvious that he did not know the routine of many
of the jobs that we did; but he let us do them, and he turned out
to be a thoughtful, polite, and damn good officer to have aboard.
The entire crew liked him."[2]

Third Class Cook John Oleksa, like many of the crew, liked the
fact that Minter was calm, fair, and willing to hear a guy out.

"Lieutenant Dial, now, he was your typical Academy man.
He was straight-faced, but he was equal to everybody. He never
misjudged a guy and did anything to, well, put anyone down. He
listened fairly. I remember this one particular time I was late, but
he took into consideration that I had helped a fellow shipmate get
back. You know, I did a good deed and I could have been in trouble
if it had been misread. He judged a person for his integrity. That's
how he was...."[3]

"Captain was a wonderful man and an inspiration. He had a
strong attitude: work hard, play hard," Richardson related. "You
couldn't help but take a liking to him right away. No one ever
thought ill of him. And he commanded our respect. He was a
strapping fellow. Must have been six feet tall and a hundred ninety
pounds, but all muscle, mind you."[4]

Chief Petty Officer William Bagwell referred to Captain Dial
as "one of the nicest officers I had ever served under. He was easy-
going and worked right alongside us. He was a man of his word."

Chief Petty Officer Bagwell remembered Captain Dial shortly
after he had taken command.

"After he arrived, I remember we were all working together
cleaning tubes in the boiler. I turned around and there he was.
He'd be in there doing it with us.... He knew each and every one
of us—there were about thirty-five of us on the ship. Together, we
ran that ship as best it could be run."[5]

The *Napa* acted as a repair ship for other vessels docked nearby
and for routine patrols. But though the ship was seaworthy, the

crew didn't always live up to the standards Minter had learned at the Academy.

"I am trying to teach them the proper way," Minter wrote to Lisa. The men didn't always make that easy.

Seaman 1st Class Paul B. "Stinky" Tardif had a slight problem with alcohol. His problem was that when he had none he was known to take some desperate action, like breaking into the pharmacist's mate's rubbing-alcohol stash and drinking the metal polish for its 50 percent alcohol content. In the middle of one particular night, he stole the *Napa*'s shore boat while she lay at anchor to make a gin run. While he was away, the *Napa* received orders to cast off. Missing their shore boat meant the *Napa* could not leave, and when Tardif finally thought to return, he noticed the stolen boat required three men to run properly. It took him a very long time to return to the *Napa*. When he did, he was met by the skipper, who confiscated the liquor, ordered Tardif below, and finally got the *Napa* underway. Nothing more was heard of the incident; but Captain Dial did parcel out the confiscated gin to all crewmen—except Tardif.

Dial also forgave Seaman 2nd Class John Oleksa when he volunteered to do some painting up on the crow's nest. As he descended with the bucket of paint, he slipped and the bucket went flying into a porthole—the skipper's porthole. Knowing Oleksa had volunteered and realizing it was an accident, Captain Dial let the incident slide.

Minter did get angry when the men were sloppy about keeping things shipshape on deck, demonstrating how he wanted things done himself and yelling if they didn't come up to snuff after being shown a time or two. "Is that the best you can do?" he'd snarl, and Oleksa remembered, "We'd get it right the next time."

Sharks were the only thing that seemed to bother Captain Dial.

"Every time we'd see them around the boat, the Old Man would issue sidearms to us and order target practice," remembered Richardson. "Any we shot would be hauled up for us to feast on that night."[6]

Minter might have shown his crew mostly patience and tolerance, but he saved his complaints for letters to Lisa:

I'm afraid that the good ship Napa isn't the best in the Navy. In fact, it is probably the worst, and is pretty much patched up and a job to keep running, but I still like it. It is hard to get organized though because being the oldest and me being the junior skipper out here, we are considered (and are) the least important unit in the fleet. We were supposed to go in for Navy Yard overhaul this month and have been making every effort to have the machinery etc. hold out until then. And now, out of a clean sky, the overhaul has been postponed indefinitely, maybe six months or more! So, we are supposed to have over 50 men on board, but had to send 10 back to the States so only have 40. We will get replacements, maybe? After everybody else has all they want! All of this isn't complaining and isn't for publication. In fact, it makes the job more interesting and tests your ingenuity. I have found so far that I know most of the answers.

Minter liked knowing the answers, even handling family budgetary matters from thousands of miles away. He worked out a household budget for Lisa and handled stock sales and dividends for his mother (who returned the favor by staying in touch with Lisa and looking out for Lisa's lack of "confidence," about which Minter seemed concerned):

Mother brought me more or less up-to-date. She said that she had received a dear letter from you telling about the life in California. She said that she knew you missed me horribly but that you are a "strong wonderful character and would carry on courageously and cheerfully as I would want you to do."

Lisa's letters to Minter from this period have been lost, and even those that got through took more than a week to arrive.

However, judging by Minter's frequent responses, Lisa wrote him often, worrying about his reaction to her going out to dinner or dancing with friends during his absence:

> I am delighted with all your activities and that you went to LA with the Mulhollands.... As far as going out is concerned, I believe it is the only thing to do under these circumstances. As long as you go in a group, I don't see any objection. I know that we both know that we would prefer to be with each other and that it will always be that way. The more I see of others, the more I love and appreciate you. You have everything and are everything I admire, respect and desire.
>
> . . .
>
> I think it is fine for you to go dancing, movies, etc. I don't believe we could ever doubt or mistrust each other. There is too much that belongs to us—alone or together. I have read many short stories and love letters since I have been here. In everyone (and every story) there is some flaw, something which prevents complete understanding between lovers. But with us, there are no flaws. I love you and trust you and believe in you.
>
> . . .
>
> ... Darling, the business about going out has, I think, worked itself out fine. As I have always said and say again, I trust you completely. I trust you with my life, as you have my heart and all the things I hold dearest in this world: you and the children. At the time I mentioned the group idea, it seemed the only possibility, as there are practically no married women here and the unmarried women won't go out with us "old fuds." My problem is simple! It would be nice if there were some married couples upon whose shoulders we could weep! I know that you cheered Bob up, and knowing how much I would appreciate the same, I couldn't possibly resent his having the pleasure of being with you.
>
> . . .

It is grand of you to branch out, meet new people. It helps to keep up your confidence.... You sounded so cheerful in this letter. It helps me to believe the things I keep telling myself about this being the best place for me—and us—right now.

Minter appeared to be putting his best face on a situation that was increasingly weighing on his spirit.

Forgot to tell you that I washed my hair so clean with Fitch's Shampoo that I uncovered a lot of gray hairs around my temples! Maybe I'll look distinguished by the time I get back!

And, more tellingly:

We are as well taken care of under the circumstances and I am the captain of a ship, and doing very interesting, congenial work. I am well and feel that I am not "wasting" all of my time. I give myself this fight talk a dozen times a day!

He worried about his crew and their families back home:

... I believe that one's spirit could easily be broken (on this station) if things at home didn't go right. It breaks my heart to see the messages every day—wives or families needing money, or sick, members of families dying and requests that so and so come home! I had a letter today from one of the men's mothers saying that she was sick and about to have an operation and that she hadn't heard from her son in 6 months and that she couldn't "rest easy" until she knew he was well. The boy promised he would write today and I wrote her a letter saying he was OK....

He worried about troubles he heard about in the fleet:

Bad news travels fast, so don't spread it. Froggy's [Tommy Warfield] ship rammed another and it was apparently his fault.

However, I believe it will be kept quiet, no one was hurt which helps. Separately, there was an explosion on one of the speed boats (a young Ensign I know, you don't, in command) and five men injured, one killed. Two general courts, going one for ships service fraud a Lt. involved (you don't know him) and one for perversion (a warrant officer) with two of '32 on the court. The more I see others' troubles, the luckier I realize we are. This Lt. Comdr. Harrison (who I said loves us dearly) told my boss that if he could only keep one ship (he has three, one much bigger and better equipped than mine) that he would prefer to keep the Napa! So!

And, after a lifetime of excelling at everything he tried, Minter worried that he wasn't doing his job well enough:

Last week at sea, I lost a motor launch.... Still don't know what will come of it, but everyone who has seen the enclosed letter seems to think that it will be passed off without too much fuss. I was so grateful that the men weren't injured, when they could have been drowned, that the unhappiness was almost overshadowed. Don't worry about it....

Minter may have not wanted Lisa to worry; but he was carrying a heavy burden, one alleviated by the vision of the "perfect family" waiting for him at home:

... Don't think for a minute that I don't have moments of despair. It sometimes seems too unfair to endure, and I want to tear my hair and scream or just plain give up. Then I start at the beginning and count our blessings and soon realize that I am the luckiest man in the world. I have you, the most perfect wife and companion any man could have and two adorable, healthy children, and a boy and a girl at that! When I write, I put everything else out of my mind, and just remember, and visualize our life together. We have come a long way together, and still have a long way to go. It helps to remember the past, ignore the present and dream of the *future*.

That future appeared increasingly at peril.

In September, a German submarine (later identified as U-652) fired on the USS *Greer*, a non-belligerent US ship, forbidden to attack Axis submarines, on patrol in the North Atlantic and based in Iceland.

When news of the encounter reached the United States, public concern ran high. In response, Germany claimed "that the attack had not been initiated by the German submarine; on the contrary... the submarine had been attacked with depth bombs, pursued continuously in the German blockade zone, and assailed by depth bombs until midnight."[7]

The message implied that the US destroyer had dropped the first depth bombs. Germany accused President Roosevelt of "endeavoring with all the means at his disposal to provoke incidents for the purpose of baiting the American people into the war."

The Navy Department answered that the German claims weren't true and that "the initial attack in the engagement was made by the submarine on the *Greer*."[8]

On September 11, 1941, President Roosevelt used the attack on the *Greer* as the topic for one of his fireside chats.[9] In Roosevelt's words:

"The *Greer* was flying the American flag. Her identity as an American ship was unmistakable. She was then and there attacked by a submarine. Germany admits that it was a German submarine. The submarine deliberately fired a torpedo at the *Greer*, followed by another torpedo attack. In spite of what Hitler's propaganda bureau has invented, and in spite of what any American obstructionist organization may prefer to believe, I tell you the blunt fact that the German submarine fired first upon this American destroyer without warning, and with the deliberate design to sink her."[10]

The president said that Germany had committed an act of piracy and announced a shoot-on-sight order. When it came to Axis submarines,

> "the very presence in any waters which America deems vital to its defense constitutes an attack. In the waters which we deem necessary for our defense, American naval vessels and American planes will no longer wait until Axis submarines lurking under the water, or Axis raiders on the surface of the sea, strike their deadly blow—first."[11]

Roosevelt explained why the United States would no longer stand by:

> "The aggression is not ours. [Our concern] is solely defense. But let this warning be clear. From now on, if German or Italian vessels of war enter the waters, the protection of which is necessary for American defense, they do so at their own peril..."[12]

Although the United States was not at war, President Roosevelt had given clear orders to attack any German or Italian vessels found in US defensive waters.

As rumors of war escalated, the undermanned and undershipped US Naval fleet made preparations to defend the Philippines. The *Napa* was assigned to net-laying and maintenance activities in Mariveles (on the southern tip of the Bataan Peninsula) and elsewhere around Manila Bay.

Though they lacked the training and even the proper equipment, the forty men (twenty fewer than was considered fully manned for active duty) did their best with what they had.

Between October 8 and December 7, the crew of the *Napa* worked hard to install anti-torpedo nets across the entrance to Mariveles Bay, never sure that they would not be attacked that day.

Minter wrote to Lisa to quell her fears. He could do little about his own:

In case anything happens out here, (and I don't believe anything will) which would prevent my writing, always remember and believe that I'll be alright. If I know you believe this, then I can have peace of mind. We belong to each other and are bound as two, which nothing can ever part? I love you, darling, more than you can ever know.

Always Minter

On December 7, the fighter pilots of the Empire of Japan bombed Pearl Harbor.

The United States—and the captain and crew of the *Napa*—were at war.

IN SEPTEMBER 2001, I was living in New York, married with two young kids (two and four years old at the time), and enjoying one of the highlights of my career as managing director of Redken Worldwide, a division of L'Oréal. It had been almost a decade since that call from Mrs. Chucker, and my investigation into my grandfather's life had continued—slowly at first; but with my present position calling for much overseas travel and a rack of frequent traveler miles, I was in the enviable position of being able to take a few side visits to further my research.

In any event, through these trips and via the many interviews conducted and books read, I had accumulated enough to write a somewhat dry but factually correct—as far as could be managed—biography of my grandfather. It was around 250 pages long and contained every single piece of information I had learned about him, including a transcription of all the letters I had come across. When time allowed, I would add little anecdotes and photos that I had come across. Where facts were unavailable, I would leave gaps. The manuscript lived on my computer, and for the moment, I was happy for it to remain there.

My father, who was living in Nice, France, came to visit us in Manhattan that September. Dinner was planned at home, on the

Upper East Side, on September 10. During that meal, I did not ever broach the topic of my research, the stories, nor the book. We had a most cordial dinner, wonderfully prepared by my wife, Yendi, and planned a Christmas get-together. Since I had to be at the office first thing the following morning, we made it an early night. My father said good night and goodbye, since he was to depart New York for London on the morning of September 12.

The following day, looking from my corner office on the nineteenth floor on Fifth Avenue and 47th Street, I had a perfect view of downtown. At around quarter to nine, I turned my head south to look out the window and saw a huge fireball in the North Tower of the World Trade Center. I called Mary Ann, my executive assistant. When she came in, I was surprised to hear her say, without missing a beat, that this was obviously a terrorist act. She had already lived through the 1993 WTC bombing.

Things quickly became a bit chaotic. Within minutes, my office was packed with members of my team who flocked to see the burning North Tower. As quickly as they had filed in, they left.

A few moments later, I was again alone in my office, looking out toward the Hudson River. I saw another plane flying south. I watched it closely. As it approached the twin towers, I imagined it was something like a Canadair, preparing to douse the flames as I had seen so many times in Corsica on rampant forest fires. The plane banked sharply right and went out of sight for me. Seconds later, the South Tower had its fireball.

I remember with crystal clarity thinking how my grandfather must have felt at the moment he learned that war had been declared. I thought of the men and women at Pearl Harbor. The parallel was absolutely evident. Once the dust had settled, even the number of casualties was similar.

My office was once again filled with my teammates. The tenor was dramatically different now. Several people were standing in tears. In a moment of clairvoyance, I remember telling a colleague that the towers would collapse. It was 9:15 a.m.

As for myself, I wanted to know the whereabouts and safety of my family. Cell service was intermittent at best. Yendi managed to locate both children. My father had been staying at a friend's place, and it took a while to reach him. By noon, the stories and tragedies began to circulate. At the kids' school, my daughter's bunkmate's father never returned. News soon followed of the loss of several people we knew, including a dear friend from Yale.

My father's plane on the twelfth was indefinitely postponed. We decided to have dinner at home again, but this time with much less formality. The ambiance in New York was somber if not outright tense. The streets of New York were remarkable for the acrid smell. They remained empty of cars, and people's faces were drawn.

At dinner that night, I felt a compulsion to tell my father every-thing—all my research, all the survivors I had tracked down, the reunions I had attended, and the first-hand accounts that professed his father's heroism. It came out, as if bottled up, in a long stream of unprepared anecdotes. There was so much to recount. I had to tell all. There was no knowing what was going to happen tomorrow.

My father listened with exceeding earnestness. At the end of dinner, after perhaps five hours of storytelling, I handed over the entire manuscript. I remember my father's look of amazement. By early morning, he had read the entire book.

It was a night that would change many things, starting with our relationship. It also profoundly changed how my father viewed his parents. Through all the years of his mother extolling his father's great courage and declaring him a hero, my father had not given any credence to the possibility that her story of his extreme valor was true. This was the evidence—researched, fact-checked, and confirmed. This was his father's life story.

WORD OF THE bombardment of Pearl Harbor reached the Phil-ippines in the early-morning hours of December 8. Carl Lee Allen, starting his 4:00 to 8:00 a.m. watch onboard the *Napa*, was the man given the news by a radioman who stopped by the boat to report the attack.

Lee didn't believe the guy.

He said, "I'll only believe you if you go right now and wake up the Old Man."

The radioman did just that.

The Old Man, Captain Minter, noted by hand in the *Napa*'s log book: "0410. Received word that hostilities with the Japanese Empire had started."

THE *NAPA* WAS anchored in nearby Olongapo (Subic Bay), north of Manila Bay. A General Quarters alarm went out, letting the men know to gather topside. When they had congregated, Captain Dial told them plainly, in a calm, firm voice, "I want you to know that hostilities have started between us and the Japanese." He paused for a moment to let the news sink in. Then he continued, "They bombed Pearl Harbor, and we are under wartime conditions. Now, let's get underway."

The men took to their stations and lost themselves for a while performing the by-now rote tasks; but as the *Napa* steamed away, each man felt his pulse racing and a slight sheen of cold sweat on his forehead. Even the skipper on the bridge, knowing his crew was looking to him to help them decide how to take the news, felt the same chill of fear deep in his stomach. But you'd never have known looking at him. Minter appeared as cool and collected as he always did. Any telltale sign of nerves from him was only observed by the very keen-eyed. Minter twisted his Annapolis class ring around and around his finger as he stared out at the open water.

Jesus, now I'll have to earn this ring, he thought. He hoped he'd prove ready.

IN THE YEARS leading up to the war, the United States fortified the Philippines as a bulwark against Japanese expansion into the

Pacific, and military authorities wrote a number of war plans to guide the defense of the islands.

The October 1940 Rainbow 5 war plan called for the United States and Philippine armies to yield the bulk of the islands to the invading Japanese troops, then fall back on and defend Manila and the critical anchorages around it. The end game was to hold out until relief could arrive from the United States.

In November of 1941, General MacArthur, whom President Franklin D. Roosevelt had placed in command of the US Army Forces in the Far East (USAFFE), was authorized to defend the Philippines. At this time, he was given notice of an alteration to the expanded role of the United States Army Air Force (AAF) in the Rainbow 5 plan. No longer would it be restricted to protecting targets in the Philippines. In the event of hostilities, the defending air forces were to carry out "air raids against Japanese forces and installations within tactical operating radius of available bases."[13]

To ready the AAF for its expanded war, the War Department planned to ship essentially all B-17s to the Islands as they came off the assembly line. Production of the then-new bombers was only getting underway, and just thirty-five B-17s had arrived in the Philippines by December 1941. Twelve more B-17s were on their way to the Philippines via Hawaii. On December 7, nineteen of the bombers were at Clark Field on Luzon, within range of bombers from Japanese-held Formosa. The remainder had been flown days before five hundred miles south, to Del Monte Field, safely out of range of Formosa-based aircraft.

Convinced that the Japanese would be unable to attack before April 1942, MacArthur was confident that the Philippines' defenses would stand tall against the assault. On December 5, 1941, in a meeting with British Adm. Tom Phillips, the commander of the Royal Navy detachment at Singapore, MacArthur spoke confidently, "The inability of an enemy to launch his air attack on these islands is our greatest security.... [N]othing would please me better than if they would give me three months and then attack here ... that would deliver the enemy into our hands."[14]

The Japanese didn't please MacArthur. They attacked three days later.

ARMY AND NAVY officers in the Philippine Islands learned about Pearl Harbor within two hours of the attack. William Manchester, in his recounting of Gen. Douglas MacArthur's life, *American Caesar,* wrote that the first official news of the attack was a phone call to Adm. Thomas Hart, the commander of the US Navy's Asiatic Fleet.

"At 0230 on the 8th (0830, 7 December, Pearl Harbor time)," about thirty-five minutes after the Pearl Harbor attack began, a Navy radioman in Manila heard the famous "This is no drill" message. He passed it to the Officer of the Day, who telephoned Admiral Hart in his room at the Manila Hotel. The ringing telephone woke Hart at "just a few minutes before" or "a few minutes after" 0300.[15]

Less than an hour and a half after Pearl Harbor was hit, Gen. George C. Marshall, US chief of staff, sent a radiogram to MacArthur. Handed to MacArthur at only 5:30 a.m., Manila time, the message stated, "Hostilities between Japan and the United States ... have commenced.... Carry out tasks assigned in Rainbow 5...."[16]

Whether this transmission reached MacArthur is still a subject of debate. The resulting catastrophe, which followed on its heels, was not.

Clearly, an attack needed to be launched before the Japanese struck. Neither that attack nor any other was forthcoming. MacArthur had denied his general's request to put the Rainbow 5 plan into action and bomb the Japanese. MacArthur said the US forces would not take the first overt action.

When the seaplane tender, *William B. Preston,* was attacked off Davao at 8:00 a.m., that point was made moot. Still, though, despite that attack, MacArthur hesitated to order an offensive. Philippine President Manuel Quezon reportedly told Maj. Gen. Dwight Eisenhower in 1942: "... MacArthur was convinced, for some strange reason, that the Philippines would remain neutral and would not be attacked by the Japanese."[17]

On the morning of December 8, there had been multiple radar sightings of enemy formations as well as false air raids. Messages and rumors were rampant, confusing, and contradictory. The P-35A and P-40 fighter squadrons had been variously scrambled to intercept incoming formations. By the standards of the day, these planes were already obsolete. They were too lightly armed and lacked armor surrounding the cockpit and self-sealing fuel tanks. Though they were scrambled that morning, it's perhaps a blessing that they had not found or engaged with the enemy, as the Japanese fighter planes, the Zeros, would have had a field day with them. The Japanese pilots, however, had other objectives in mind. Throughout the morning, the bombers were kept in a defensive mode and carried no bombs. The remaining B-17s were scrambled to avoid being caught on the ground in the early hours of the 8th. They were sent out to patrol the waters without fighter cover. At 9:10 a.m., it was recorded that fifty-four US airplanes were in the air, with just thirty-six held back in reserve. At 11:00 a.m., with no apparent incoming attack, the "all-clear" was given and all US planes on patrol were ordered back to base.[18]

Not all factors can be accounted for when it comes to battle and, in this instance, it seemed as though the very heavens themselves conspired to propel the Japanese Empire to victory. Weather itself, in the strangest of ways, skewed the odds entirely in Japan's favor.

A heavy fog blanketed Luzon and played a critical role in delaying any major offensive by the Japanese. Initially, the Japanese had planned a coordinated air attack on the Philippines in conjunction with the Pearl Harbor attack; however, because of inclement weather, Japanese military leaders were obliged to put that plan on hold. Once the fog had lifted, five hours after news of Pearl Harbor had arrived, the only working radar on the Philippine Islands (at Iba Airfield) showed that at least thirty Japanese aircraft were flying south over Luzon, headed for God-knows-where.[19]

Three ready US fighter squadrons were again scrambled, each commanded to patrol a specific area. The 17th went to cover Bataan, while the 21st flew over Manila. The 34th squadron from Del Carmen was ordered to patrol Clark Airfield, to give cover to the 20th, which was on the ground refueling. However, because of a thick haze of dust that consumed Del Carmen airfield, the 34th was delayed in taking off. The delay would have fatal consequences.

The 3rd Pursuit Squadron at Iba (thirty-seven miles to the west of Clark) scrambled but failed to engage with the enemy. They flew back to base and were caught by surprise on their approach for landing.

All the remaining aircraft in Luzon were on the ground, being serviced or standing ready for takeoff. The pilots of the 20th Pursuit Squadron at Clark were at lunch with the B-17 pilots from the 19th Bombardment Group (BG).

Every outward appearance of a normal peacetime day in the FEAF (Far East Air Force) disappeared at 11:27 a.m. The aircraft that the Iba radar had picked up over the Lingayen Gulf, on the west coast of Luzon, appeared "out of the blue" over Clark Air Base.

Japanese bombs began to fall at about 12:35 p.m. One B-17 navigator reported, "The first notice we had at the 19th BG Headquarters was when someone screamed, 'Here they come!' "

Fifty minutes after the first bombs started to fall on Clark, the Japanese flew back to their base in Formosa, leaving Americans confronting death and wounds, destruction, damage, and demoralization. The Japanese had destroyed half the B-17s and one-third of all the P-40s in the Philippines. Two of the four P-40 pursuit squadrons were eliminated as combat units. Though all of its planes had not been destroyed, the 5th Pursuit Squadron, the

34th, equipped with outdated P-35As, had also been eliminated from the war. Its pilots knew, after watching the attack, that to match their planes against the Japanese bombers was suicide.

The Filipinos themselves, citizens and army scouts alike, watched events unfolding with an increasing sense of impending doom. In what must have seemed like jumping from the frying pan into the fire, they realized that having put all their energies toward fighting for independence from one overlord (the United States), they now faced the grim prospect of allying with them to ward off another invader.

Two days later, on December 10, the Japanese bombed and strafed Nichols and Del Carmen Fields (fifteen miles south of Clark), leaving those bases in shambles and destroying about half the remaining P-40s and all but five of the P-35As. Three days after war's start, the Japanese had eliminated US airpower from the Philippines at the trifling cost of a few of their aircraft and crews. The Empire had dealt a crippling blow on its first pass. Minter, the crew of the *Napa*, and every airman, soldier, and sailor in the Philippines knew they were in for the fight of their lives.

— 6 —

WHEN ANY MILITARY man went to war, his family back at home went with them. Hungry for any news, the wives, mothers, and fathers of those fighting men spent nights gathered around their radios, followed every frame of the newsreels shown at the neighborhood cinema, bought more newspapers than in recorded history, and exchanged every scrap of information—correct or not—on the course of the war.

Mothers knitted socks, wives handed out coffee at the USO, Hollywood stars performed on "Buy Bonds" tours, boys played soldiers with the villains then called "krauts or nips," people cheerfully rationed gas and scrap metal and rubber, and everyone prayed and lived for letters from their loved ones.

Lisa was no exception.

Even before news of Pearl Harbor broke, Lisa was a dutiful correspondent—writing daily, imparting cheerful snippets of her life and the children's, providing gossip about shared acquaintances, giving thanks for gifts from Minter sent long ago and finally received, and, always, expressions of her love.

Darling, darling, darling!
    Just as I was reading your letter—adoring the pictures of you (and) a package from you! Tore it open—wept over the precious

note—and died with joy over the bag and slipcovers! Angel, they're beautiful! I'm mad about them! Got so excited with so much happening all at once that I could hardly stand it! Then I finished your letter and got excited all over again!... My, it's fun to get letters from you! I'm so happy after my big morning I could scream! Now I won't be able to settle down all day! I'll just read your letter and pore over the pictures and finger the bags—and walk on clouds!... Now your daughter with her beautiful brown eyes like her father's must have her lunch and her nap. So I'm off, till tomorrow...

. . .

Diana is starting to talk!! She says, "Do walk" (go walk) and "baby" and "daddy." Isn't that thrilling? She's always been a lady.... Vic has had to learn to control his emotions—and still keep his fire. He's wonderful.... [He's] no prodigy (though I think he could be if we taught him?!), but he has infinite common sense—and I much prefer that...

. . .

Vic watches over Diana like a hawk. Not allowing her to stray for an instant. He is a very dependable little fellow—reliable. When the ball goes into the street, he comes to tell me to get it.... He has become very proficient at entertaining himself—very self-reliant. Wait till you hear him sing "God Bless America"—it's wonderful! It gets me, truly. And he carries the tune! All tunes!...

But running just beneath the sunny surface of her letters was Lisa's increasing wistfulness. She loved her children, but single parenthood proved hard for her.

... Of course, [Victor] still has some moments, but don't we all? And he can be exceedingly strenuous at times!... He talks of you a great deal. He's reached the stage where he asks "why" about everything we tell him!

Nonetheless, she longed for the day Minter would return and they could add to their little family.

The woman next door... came home from the hospital last night with her baby girl, and it gave me such a pang! I seem to be affected by things so easily lately. I suppose when you've more or less "run the gauntlet" of human emotions you do feel them more keenly. I watched them for a long time in their lighted nursery.... It made me want another baby! Can you bear it?

In late November, the approach of the holidays made Lisa ever more aware of how lonely she was and how sad the season was without Minter:

... The streets downtown are filled with Christmas decorations— lighted trees on lampposts and garlands and wreaths and bells. All very festive and gay and crowded. And almost made me Christmasy—even though I didn't think it could be done. This is the second Christmas we will have been apart. Remember the other? I'll miss you darling.
I love you so.
Lisa

A line in a letter received from Minter (now lost) caused a tremor of fear to rip through Lisa and she reacted strongly in her reply:

In the last paragraph you said, "In case anything happens to pre-vent my writing—" Oh, my darling, it mustn't, it mustn't. But I know, I'll try hard to know you are alright. I'll remember that you love me always. I never want you to worry about us! You have enough on your mind without that. We are one and neither time nor circumstance can ever separate us. We both know that. Trust and faith and love like ours is so terribly great and beau-tiful.... Oh, my darling, if I could only reach across the water and touch your hands. If I could take them in mine and look into your eyes and tell you how I love you!

Lisa wrote, on the night of December 6, of a dream she had that showed a trace of prescience, as the *Napa* was to earn some honors in the coming days:

Dearest,

Last night I had the most wonderful dream! I dreamed that you came home. Oh, the joy and happiness of it—it was glorious. I reveled in it. I showed you proudly all the things I had done and Vic was so thrilled to have you back. I asked you about the boat and you said you'd gotten a letter of condemnation about it. I was furious. It was all so real. I feel as though it happened! But it was awful hard when I realized it was only a dream and wouldn't come true for a long, long time. So I feel kinda let down today...

Lisa's letdown would soon turn to horror as she heard of the devastating attack on Pearl Harbor and the bombing of Clark Field. She grabbed her pen with shaking hand to write:

... Ah, Minter, Minter, I have just heard on the radio of the attacks on Manila. Oh god—I am lost. Where are you, how are you? Darling be brave. It's horrible. I am so sorry for you. And I'll be brave too. It's something we've got to face—and we can— we must. Oh darling, I know you'll be alright. I know it. They have called back, on the radio—all the Fort McArthur men and the Terminal Island aviators and the Navy District men. We're standing by too, you see. You are not alone, my love. Always be brave—don't be afraid ever. I'm right there beside you, and my love is an armor nothing can pierce! You are enveloped in it—remember that! Nothing can ever happen to you until I stop loving you—and that day will never come. You are my one love forever.

You may never get this letter now, but I am counting on your knowing that we are all well, as you are counting on my knowing about you. I didn't think this would happen. I was so sure they would keep peace. I almost can't believe it—and feel stunned. My thoughts are of you every moment. Are you tired my darling? From no sleep and the strain? Oh, if I could only comfort you and hold you in my arms. Remember that the source of your power is the same one that makes the wind blow—and the seas roll. It is infinite—never ending. You can never be tired if you know that. Keep alert—and be a good captain. Oh my dearest—I can't write any more now.

 I love you too much,

 Lisa

     . . .

My dearest love,

 Heaven knows how or when this will reach you, but it's a try, anyway.

 I want you to know we are well and safe, of course. My thoughts are with you every moment of my life, and now the first shock is over, we are calm and ready for anything . . .

     . . .

  . . . After the news on Sunday that Manila had not been bombed yet, I began to live again. And now I know they can't take you by surprise, and you will be alright. I know it, I feel it. I know too, what a horrible nightmare you must be going through. But you are equal to it—more than anyone else. The radio keeps us informed of all that they can possibly tell us—and we've heard of all the air raids you've had . . . .

She longed to hear from Minter and yet did so only three times between December of 1941 and February of 1942. Even though communications home were now heavily censored, she savored every word. The first was a telegram, which allowed Lisa to release the breath she felt she had been holding since word reached her, and the rest of the country, of the attack on Pearl Harbor.

WESTERN UNION Dec 14, 1941
SAFE AND SOUND. EVERYTHING WILL BE ALRIGHT. CHIN
UP. WIRE MOTHER. ALL MY LOVE.
MINTER DIAL ASIATIC STATION

It assured her that at least Minter was still safe, for which she was very grateful; but it again used the phrase she would come to hate: "Keep your chin up." How was she to do that when she could barely sleep for worry and had to watch carefully not to transfer her tightly controlled hysteria to the children? They were like little barometers, ready to rise or fall at her slightest expression of fear. She had to be brave for them when all she really felt like doing was screaming. Little Victor was already old beyond his years, trying to be the man of the family in his Daddy's absence and actually comforting Lisa by reassuring her that Daddy would be home soon. She couldn't add more to his burden or Minter's. She would keep a positive outlook, at least in her dealings with the children and in her letters to Minter. At night, alone in the bed they had shared, things were different, and she let the fears come and the tears flow. But it would all be "chin up" in the letters.

Minter, aware now that he and his men were in the midst of a situation that was bleak and getting bleaker, obviously decided much the same. Lying to the ones at home became the sailor's and soldier's burden. You lied because you loved them. Minter's own letters to Lisa were a perfect demonstration of this.

December 1941
Sweetheart darling,
I have been sitting here reveling in the joy of looking at the pictures of you, Victor and Diana. This is a luxury for which I have little time these days. To know that I have you is the inspiration I need, however, and I am more than grateful for it.
We have just finished a very fine turkey dinner with olives, cranberries, apple pies, cheese and all! I'm keeping up my

dieting and exercise but miss the golf, tennis and riding. I'm in better physical condition now than I have been in for years.

I'm about out of clean clothes, so today I ran across those fancy blue striped skivvies and am now all dressed up!

I hope my Christmas presents arrived OK. They were mailed 29 November and were insured so let me know if they don't arrive. Your package hasn't arrived and I'm crushed. I wanted so much to see the pictures and hear your voices. Maybe they'll get here yet! Give Diana and Victor special Christmas hugs for me and always remember that you are my inspiration and guiding star, "a sailor's wife, a sailor's star shall be."

Don't worry, because I want you to be more beautiful than ever (not really possible) when I get back.

Whenever I cable you, please wire mother automatically.

Remember that all the ways of saying it, mean the same "I love you."

Minter

He did let a slight inkling of his true feelings emerge in that same letter, one that, no doubt, his wife would have found ominous.

My mental condition is as well as could be expected under the circumstances. I am particularly grateful that we bought the house and have our affairs as well in order as they are.

WHILE MINTER FOUGHT to reassure Lisa with his cheerful missives, Lisa had a different approach to supporting her man, spinning what would be a recurring thread through her letters— that the love she and Minter shared would prove a talisman against danger, providing Minter protection against injury or death. Faced with a terrifying situation over which she had no control, Lisa, never before religious, called upon a spiritual power she fervently hoped would take care of her husband.

But there is a power, higher than any mortal power that guides us and protects us—keeps us safe from harm. And that is the power we must rely on. Life will be more beautiful than ever after all this is over and we are together again. This is another testing field for us, and we must prove ourselves.

. . .

... Oh my love, it's so hard to be nonchalant when tragedy stalks our lives. Know how I love you and ache for you dearest. And know that I am perfectly certain that you are alright—and that one of these fine days you will come home to me. I am not worrying—but I am so sorry for you. I've come to love the nights because they are your mornings. And I think there is such a secure feeling in daylight—and I'm always glad when your nights are over. Remember the armor of my love that you're wearing. Nothing can pierce it. Nothing. This is a terrible thing, but thank god we are able to meet it. I love you more, if that's possible, than I ever did before.

While the Navy, like all branches of the armed forces, joined with the media in imploring families to write to their men as often as possible, emphasizing the keen importance of these communications to the morale of those at war, the sad fact was that the system for delivering mail to those stationed overseas was not as reliable as the love and support of military families. This letter, like all of those Lisa wrote to Minter between December and April 1942, was returned—undeliverable.

Without Minter, her rock, to allay her fears, and with all her mental energy focused on reassuring the children, Lisa faced sleepless nights during which all her fears rushed in on her alone in her room.[1] Exhausted and in emotional pain, having to deal with the needs of two small children, Lisa was suffering. To coax her through the pain, Lisa took more frequently an extra tumbler. And, at times, there was another one before bed to help her achieve a fitful sleep.

As Lisa drank more, she wrote less. Each returned letter made her more fragile, and she barely dared hope that Minter was alive and unharmed. Her frail emotional restraint was shattered when she finally received a telegram from Minter saying he was safe. She believed that all her desperate bargaining prayers with God had been answered. Lisa went from the depths to the heights in an instant:

> Oh my love, my dearest *love*,
>
> How beautiful are the footsteps of the messenger of good news! Your telegram came this morning. The boy asked me to open it in front of him, and with trembling hands, I did. Then I read the words—"Safe and Sound"!! Oh darling—you were safe, safe, safe!!! Thank god. I almost kissed the boy! Then your reassuring "everything will be alright." And I knew it would, because you said so. You have always calmed me by that phrase, you always will. The tears rolled merrily down my cheeks! I rushed to phone Mother and Vic (who had spent the night at her house) and Mother wept too! Then I wired your Mother. Then I called Dot and John—and they wept too! Then Mother called Connie and yes, she wept too!... Not a dry seat in the house!... It was a glorious day! I'm going to frame the wire, dearest, and hang it right over the desk to cheer me every moment. "Everything will be alright." I can hear you say it, and feel your strength .... I wanted to let you know it had come, and how thankful I was. But they have stressed keeping everything clear for official messages.
>
> ... Now I've heard from you, I can begin to live again—new hope, new life. But my heart is with you in this ordeal you're going through, and probably will continue to go through for a long time. I am by your side for always, Minter. Hold my hand and keep going *forward* .....
>
> For always and *forever* your adoring wife, Lisa.

The news cheered more than Lisa. Minter's family, hungry for news, was elated to hear that he was safe. A letter from his half-sister, Laura Emily, was also returned, but shows us how well-loved Minter was:

> Dearest Minter,
> ... From Lisa, [I received] the first news from my dear brother for some time. As you have always known I am proud of you and rejoice with you over the great progress you have made. You are giving your all in this great crisis, as we Americans must do.... My emotions are too deep for words. This message cannot express all I wish to say. I love you so much. God bless you and keep you every moment.
> Devotedly, Laura Emily

Lisa, like everyone else, stuck close to her radio, particularly when the national news was broadcast three times a day. She also avidly read the daily papers and joined the estimated fifty million Americans who watched the biweekly newsreels at the local theaters. These short dramatic newsreels employed some of Hollywood's finest filmmakers, and the US Government's Office of War Information (OWI) kept the public informed of the war's progress through them. They did not show the whole story of what was going on in the war, though.[2] The OWI carefully monitored what stories were featured. "Anchors Aweigh" or "The Marine Hymn" played thrillingly in the background, and though American troops might be said to have "sustained some casualties," the baritone-voiced narrator always assured the audience that such events "didn't stop our boys."

More than thirty government agencies were involved in censorship, and government control of the media was comprehensive. All news about the war had to pass through the OWI. The government also relied heavily on reporters' patriotism, which ensured that, in their dispatches from the front lines, they tended to accentuate the positive. John Steinbeck explained how he and other reporters went about their work:

"The rules for correspondents [were both]... imposed and self-imposed.... There were no cowards in the American Army, and of all the brave men, the private in the infantry was the bravest and noblest. The reason for this in terms of the War Effort was obvious. The infantry private had the dirtiest, weariest, least rewarding job in the whole war. In addition to being dangerous, a great many of the things he had to do were stupid. He must therefore be reassured that these things he knew to be stupid were actually necessary and wise, and that he was a hero for doing them.... A second convention held that we had no cruel or ambitious or ignorant commanders....

"We were all a part of the War Effort. We went along with it, and not only that, we abetted it. Gradually it became a part of all of us that the truth about anything was automatically secret and that to trifle with it was to interfere with the War Effort. By this I don't mean that the correspondents were liars... [but] it is in the things not mentioned that the untruth lies.

"We felt responsible to what was called the home front. There was a general feeling that, unless the home front was carefully protected from the whole account of what war was like, it might panic. Also, we felt we had to protect the armed services from criticism, or they might retire to their tents to sulk like Achilles."[3]

Such benign propaganda was helpful to mollify the sharpest edges of the crushing anxiety felt by the wives and mothers, but it couldn't still the constant drumbeat of worry. Fear of telegrams was ever-present, and everyone worriedly scanned newspapers for the columns of names of the fallen—sons, brothers, husbands, those who were never coming home.

Lisa was among these hollow-eyed readers. Her chin was dutifully pointed upwards, but it was surely quivering.

Remember always how terribly much I love you. Just wait till I get you home—you're never going to leave me again. Never.

Won't it be fun!? We can live on a farm—buy a horse, and settle down, and let the rest of the world go by. I'm serious.

Ah, there's so much I want to say, but I can't without letting down the bars. I love you so. Take care of yourself.

Your own, Lisa

Women stateside took on unfamiliar roles as they became involved in the war effort. Nineteen-year-old Geraldine Hoff became a factory worker, a job from which she would be immortalized as "Rosie the Riveter." And Lisa acted as plane spotter on the roof of the Pacific Coast Club where she and Minter had met:

> Every six days, Dorothy and Eleanor Campbell and I have a two-hour duty on the roof of the PC Club reporting all planes to Army headquarters. It makes me feel I'm doing something. But it is so little. I wish I could help build a ship or a plane to fight with.
> ... Today is my duty day! ... I'm not allowed to tell where our Post is—we moved from the Club. We have sealed orders to be opened if our Post is disabled, and we are to defend it with our lives. It sounds exciting, but it really isn't that dangerous! I think there is very little possibility now of an attack here.

But, despite such distractions, without Minter—who was truly her rock and on whom she depended for strength and financial and emotional security—Lisa was unraveling. She wrote not only of peace as a cessation of war, but as something she longed for in her own soul. She tried hard to keep such anguish from her children, so the bottle was her only solace.

> ... Oh my precious, how I long for you. It's so hard to be brave all the time! If I could only know where you are now—and how you are. Every now and then I get a feeling that you're very near—that you're coming home—it's glorious while it lasts, but the letdown when it can't be true is hideous. Sometimes in the night I waken

to hear funny little noises in the bed beside me—and I think you've come back, but of course, it's always Vicky, doing his best to take your place. Someday, this will all be over and we'll be happy, together again—and when that day comes, you'll never leave me again. I swear it. Never, never, never. You won't even be allowed your accustomed privacy in the bathroom, chum! Or have you ever had it? We'll live somewhere—simply, and the children will grow up and be off—and we'll have each other at long last, alone and forever. Then there'll be the grandchildren coming home for Christmas, and quiet nights when we'll talk about our youth—to each other—because no one else will listen. But, oh how wonderful the peace will be. In mind and body...

With no word from her husband, Lisa turned to memories and dreams to keep her sanity:

... It's almost 1942—will be when you read this. Oh god, I pray that this year will bring peace. Ten years ago, you graduated from the Naval Academy. Eight years ago you married me. This new year must bring us much happiness to compete with the years that we have known. I'll count on that—you must too. It will give us something to look for, day by day. I'll live for the day when I'll hear your step, and your whistle in the hall—to know that you've come home. Come home to stay. Wherever you are, my love, have courage and take care of yourself for us. We always need you so.

Your own adoring Lisa

By the end of December 1941, the Japanese had successfully invaded many islands and countries throughout the Pacific. From the Americans, they took Guam and Wake Island, southeast from Japan. From the British, they took Hong Kong and the Gilbert Islands and had invaded British Burma, Borneo, and Malaya. Up north, they had taken Attu in the Bering Sea, west of Alaska. Most important for Minter, the Japanese had also assaulted the northern Philippines and met little resistance.

My darling Minter,
   I have dreamed of you three times since you've been gone.
   The first time the night before the attack on Pearl Harbor—when I thought you had come home and all was happiness and joy. The second time was the night before I read in the paper of the evacuation of Cavite (headquarters of the United States Asiatic Fleet in the Philippines). That time you were in a blue uniform and blue cap cover. You were driving the car and you looked straight ahead, not at me, and said, "This is very serious, Lisa." Then, the night before last I dreamed again that you had come home, and such joy was never known before! It is hard to waken to realities after that.

. . .

Yesterday, the blouse arrived. Oh, it's beautiful! And, oh, it was contact again with you!... It's been so long. If it weren't for that telegram hanging over my desk, I'd get discouraged...

. . .

... We mustn't forget in the present to look to the future. The silver lining is brilliant—the dark clouds will pass. The skies are blue behind them—and are only temporarily hidden, but they are there. Remember we are hand in hand forever. I am always beside you. I love you so!
   Lisa

. . .

My very dearest love,
   A month ago today your wire came! What a wonderful day that was. I'm still reading and still believing it: "everything will be alright." How I wonder where you are.

Lisa felt that the world she had built with Minter was collapsing around her, and this feeling was underscored when the man who had introduced them and served as head usher at their wedding succumbed to cancer.

Precious,

Charlie Keene died of cancer of the lung last Friday. Isn't that sad... Charlie was such a good friend, a sincere one.... My chin is just about worn out from trying to stay up—it needs a boost! How's yours, angel?

. . .

My very dearest darling,

... Here it is March—our month—already! Two wonderful days in it. The 21st your birthday and the 24th our eighth anniversary. We're growing up, pet. Spring is at hand again!... Spring is such a happy, hopeful time of year... We've been together eight Aprils now, waiting for the green on the swaying willow bough. Dearest, next Spring, we'll celebrate! I'm sure of it.... Ah, Time, for God's sake, fly! I love you so that my heart aches from the fullness. You know that I am completely yours.

Lisa

But both the birthday and wedding anniversary mentioned in that letter were spent without Minter; and those around Lisa, seeing how fragile the constant strain and loneliness had made her, tried to buck her up.

My dearest love,

Our week has come and gone! More milestones! On your birthday we woke up singing to you then we went to the beach for the morning.... Dot gave a sit-down dinner for us—you and me—for our anniversary! There were 11 of us—you were the 12th. I missed you dearest.

... The 23rd I got an air mail letter from Dorothy saying that a friend of yours and hers in the Navy had just called her and told her that he just heard that you were safe and well! Could

give no details as to where you were though or anything!...
[T]hat was such good news!

... Then I got a post card from Ruffin [Cox], with a picture
of Point Loma on it saying that he wanted to see us all soon and
that he'd call at the first opportunity. I nearly died! Maybe you'll
be seeing him too before long. He is so much a part of our early
life that it will be almost like seeing part of you again.

Today Diana and I are sitting outdoors in our bathing suits.
Shades of Annapolis! Oh dearest—I'm so hungry for you. I love
you more every day—every moment! I can scarcely wait till we
settle down on a farm—and I'll never, never let you out of my
sight again! Now I'm off to air duty! My dearest, dearest love. I
adore you.

Lisa

Lisa thought her children only saw the brave face she was trying so hard to keep in place; but, like all children of alcoholics,
they had the terrifying experience of seeing Lisa lose control, both
of her drinking and her tears, and they had certainly heard her sob
alone in her room at night. Such experiences made Diana timid
and fearful and had the opposite, but no less detrimental effect,
on young Victor. He strove hard to keep things under control, be
the man of the house, and comfort his mother:

I wish you could have seen your stalwart little son when I cried
because he was singing Happy Birthday to your picture that Sat.
He put my head on his shoulder and said, "Don't cry, Mommy.
Daddy doesn't like cryings. Be a happy girl!" Minter's own son.
Fight hard for him, darling. Because, he's worth it.

I love you so, Lisa

In April of 1942, the emotional merry-go-round spun again,
and three letters, long delayed, at last arrived together from
Minter.

Adorable,

How are you and our precious family getting along? Even though I haven't heard from you since the war started and may not for some time I know that you are doing your part by keeping the home fires burning.

Ever attentive, Minter managed the financial matters from a distance.

I got a pay increase of $20.00.... I registered an additional allotment of $20.00 a month which you should get around the 1st of March. The main reason for doing this was to let you know I was o.k. at that time.... If you can save any of it—it will help pay mother the $300.00 (plus 4% interest from Feb. 1941) which I owe her.

Now that they aren't making any more cars, I am doubly glad we bought the Lincoln when we did. Hope it is standing up.

There were tender thoughts about the children.

[I] framed the large picture of you and the children in a double frame with the one of you in the wedding dress. It makes a "contrived story" with the title "Before and After Marriage"!? How are the children?

When they exasperate you beyond control (as they used at times to do to us both) think of what I would give to be there "to be exasperated!"

And encouragement for the future.

Try as I do not to worry. Make the best of the situation and trust the ultimate outcome. As you know, all letters are censored—and mail is irregular. Remember that no news is good news and please don't worry.

Lisa was over the moon to receive them:

My very dearest darling,

Three letters from you!! Oh you can never know what they
have done for me. Now I know that I had just been living in a
kind of daze and now I'm almost human again. I've read and
re-read them so much already that they are very nearly worn
to shreds!

... Darling, your Christmas presents never arrived—but you
never can tell, they might turn up. I'm sorry you didn't get ours.
We love you so terribly hard—we're living for the day you'll
come home to us. God grant it will be soon.

Your adoring, Lisa

. . .

My dearest, dearest love,

My heart is so full—and I don't ever know how to tell you
what I feel. Knowing where you are—and that you are safe is the
most wonderful relief! But the hardships you must be, and will
be, enduring from here on in bother me so. What is the answer I
wonder? That's a silly question! There is only one answer—faith.
We've got to have it. I know you'll be alright—all of you there
somehow....

Lisa wrote of measles and money matters; but they were trifles
compared to the ever-present terror she felt and refused to face—
that Minter might not be coming home.

Those are the minor details—there are so many things to be
thankful for. You are safe and well is the most important thing
in our lives. Yesterday, Vic saw a sailor on the street and said,
"Will you please go and get my Daddy? We're awful lonesome
to see him. And when he comes home I'm going to hug him so
hard he can never get away again." The sailor had tears in his
eyes as he stooped and said, "I'll find him, son." I loved him. Vic

was satisfied. He turned his cheery, bright little face up to mine and said, "He'll be home soon, Mommy." If anything or anyone upsets me, he always comes to my aid with, "Oh, that bad man! I'm going to take his panties down and lambaste *him* on his bare bottom." My protector. And Diana, my *sweet*, feminine, dainty, gentle little Diana! Who could be richer than we? Blessed with our two darlings! They are definitely worth fighting for, my love. And they adore you. I do too, you know! Or had you heard, that I will love you forevermore, and forever more and more. It's true. Remember our life together—and think of our future yet to be lived, and nothing can stop us. Nothing.

Your own, Lisa

But, of course, something could stop them—a world at war.

By the time Lisa received those three letters from Minter in April of 1942, Japanese forces had occupied the naval and air bases of southern Indochina. The Philippines were almost completely occupied.

The Philippines Campaign was coming to a seemingly inevitable conclusion. By March, the bulk of the remaining Allied troops were either cornered on the Bataan Peninsula or were pinned in on the Island of Corregidor. The ensuing battles over the next two months would feature some of the most brutal fighting yet to happen. The fall of Bataan and the battle for Corregidor lay ahead, with the odds heavily stacked against them. For Minter and the American servicemen left behind, an inconceivable fresh hell awaited them.

— 7 —

A general is just as good or just as bad as
the troops under his command make him.

GEN. DOUGLAS MACARTHUR

T HE *NAPA* WAS no longer just a slightly rusty old tugboat. Despite having only two 3-inch, 50-caliber dual-purpose guns and one .30-caliber Lewis machine gun—all leftovers from WWI—as the war heated up, the ship was called to undertake anti-aircraft duty.

The crew was handicapped in this by the difficulty of manually gauging the height of the Japanese bombers (which were generally out of range) and the timing needed to possibly hit any target with a degree of certainty. Using elderly fuses to set off the *ack-ack* cartridges was also imprecise work. Sometimes they went off, sometimes they didn't.

The *Napa*'s cook, John Oleksa, was pressed into duty as a gun loader, and Chief Petty Officer William Wells earned the nickname of "Gunner" for his expertise in manning his gun. He had to guess at the length of time needed to set the fuses and adjust as he went along. This usually meant that when an eight-second release didn't work, Wells tried a ten-second one, but the targeted plane was often long gone by the time the fuse actually ignited the ammo.

Another uncontrolled explosion had tragic consequences. The *Napa* had been trying to save oil, using less and running the engine hot. The boiler blew one afternoon and, unsure if there had been an attack, Wells sounded the general alarm. When the smoke cleared, the crew ran down the hatch to discover there had been an explosion in the boiler room. Three crewmen had been badly injured. Fireman Pitts died the day of the explosion; Benny Bisente, a Filipino 2nd Class Water Tender, died the following day; and 2nd Class Water Tender Austin Murdock suffered severe burns.

One had to imagine the weight of responsibility that Minter felt at having such casualties on his watch. These would have been his first letters written to family members announcing the death of his crewmembers.

The incident heightened the fear each crewmember felt in the pit of his stomach; but no man mentioned it to another, and each looked toward the captain for how to act during what was rapidly becoming a crisis. Minter set his jaw, hid his fears, and did his job. So did his crew. The men of the *Napa* fought on.

In an attempt to arm themselves with something more than the outdated weaponry they had, Gunner Wells led a raid on the ammo depot on the island. The Japanese bombing had devastated the area but had miraculously missed the depot. Wells knew where the .50-caliber machine guns were stored, so he shot the lock off the door. The men grabbed an air-cooled .50-caliber and the fittings they figured they might need. When the team got it back to the ship, the ship-fitter and Wells rigged up a mount and put the gun on the forecastle between the two 3-inch 50s. Then they kept on shooting.

The *Napa* fought back in other ways, too. With no more air cover since the American air force in the Philippines had been annihilated by the Japanese attack, the US Navy ships found getting into port to refuel a venture fraught with danger. As a result, many boats left the area or were scuttled under orders from Command. Once they had cleared the area, the *Napa* was charged with laying down mines in the various bays to deny the enemy entrance. The crew laid more than thirteen thousand mines, a hazardous exercise as many of the mines had been issued during WWI and were unstable. Captain Dial found himself thanking some unseen God every night his crew didn't blow themselves up. It seemed luck was on their side.[1]

That luck would soon turn.

The Battle of Bataan was about to begin. It would be known as "the American Thermopylae."[2]

THE *NAPA* HAD a front-row seat when the Japanese bombers took a run at the USS *Peary*, a Clemson-class destroyer. The *Peary* had been hidden in Campomanes Bay on Negros Island, where her crew had camouflaged her with green paint and palm fronds, hoping to elude Japanese patrol bombers. The next morning, a Japanese bomber spotted the *Peary* making her way out of the bay and shadowed her until early afternoon, when other bombers joined in a two-hour attack. Gunner Wells would later say it was one of the most spectacular things that he had ever seen, a remarkable feat of ship handling.

The USS *Peary* was in the middle of the Bay when the bombing started, and fortuitously it had plenty of water in which to maneuver. There were seven bombers in the formation, and they made numerous runs attempting to hit the ship, but the *Peary* zigged and zagged to evade the bombs.

During the final Japanese bomber run, the *Peary* was running straight when she began to smoke. The *Napa* crew thought she was hit and maybe out of action. Suddenly they saw the destroyer stop and reverse course to back herself into the smoke, stymieing the bomber pilots searching for a target. As bombs rained down, the *Peary* emerged from the smoke not ten feet from where the bombs had hit the water. The bombers, having dropped their last loads, peeled off, and the *Peary* stopped her engines and laid to. The *Napa* raced to give assistance.

Pulling alongside, Minter grabbed the megaphone and hailed the captain of the *Peary*, Cdr. J.M. Bermingham.

"Do you need any help?" Minter bellowed.

"No, thanks. We made it through with no wounded," came Bermingham's reply. "We don't need any help. But I believe we have to do a lot of laundry!"

Minter and the crew laughed long and hard about that answer, knowing how close it had been to having an entirely different outcome. The men of the *Napa* stored what they had learned about evasive tactics from the *Peary*, too. They'd need that knowledge sooner than they'd know.

FUEL WAS RUNNING short, and even access to it was becoming challenging. Letting the better-equipped boats pass in front of them, the *Napa* made it to the fuel pumps after seeing the others off safely. Barely taking time to tie up to the dock, the crew raced to pump the fuel when they heard the dreaded drone of airplane engines above them, closing fast on their location. Dive bombers sporting the unmistakable Rising Sun emblem broke cloud cover and opened fire on the *Napa*. With fuel still spilling out of the hose, Minter ordered the *Napa* to make a run for it. The crew cast off the ropes and dove onto the deck, and the boat roared out into the bay, zigging and zagging as the *Peary* had done before them to avoid getting hit.

Once safe, Minter ordered that all the fuel from every possible source be collected, and, in an effort to save the boat and his men, asked permission of Admiral Hart, commander-in-chief of the Asiatic fleet, to set sail for Australia. Hart refused, explaining his thinking by pointing out to Minter that the *Napa*'s top cruising speed of ten knots would have made it a sitting duck for the

Japanese submarines. He ordered the *Napa* to remain and continue laying mines and performing emergency tasks as needed.

It was only a matter of time before the *Napa* ran out of fuel. In fact, it was the last USN ship in operation in Manila Bay. Once fuel ran out, only a skeleton crew was kept on board to man the guns as the Japanese continued to bomb Cavite Bay. On March 18, 1942, Minter was relieved of his command and was ordered onshore as secretary and liaison officer to Capt. Kenneth Hoeffel, the highest-ranking Naval officer remaining in the 16th Naval District. Minter was given this important assignment because many of the Army's communication capabilities had been lost in previous bombing raids. Naval communications, still operational due to their location inside the Queen's Tunnel on Corregidor, were therefore irreplaceable and needed to be organized and maintained at all costs.[3]

Less than a month later, under continued bombing attacks, with no fuel with which to escape and nowhere to run, the valiant crew of the fierce little tug-turned-mine-layer-turned-destroyer was ordered to abandon ship, and the *Napa* was scuttled. A fighter to the end, she took forty-eight hours to sink.

FOR FOUR GRUELING months preceding the scuttling of the *Napa*, the US troops on Bataan, a peninsula jutting out into Manila Bay, had been fighting in some of the most horrific conditions ever endured. Cornered on the end of the peninsula and without hope of resupply, the troops were running low on ammunition, and their mess kits were long emptied of even hardtack. They had been subsisting on a diet that had grown progressively more bizarre. At first the men ate "cavalry steak," the horses that had been used to help carry supplies. Then they joined their fellow soldiers, the Filipinos, in eating any dog they could catch, then monkeys, cats, rats, and snakes. Finally, they were reduced to eating slugs and silkworms. With such a diet came diseases caused by a lack of vitamins, such as scurvy and beriberi, and others such as amoebic and bacillary dysentery, typhus, typhoid, and gas gangrene, which passed infection from one man's wounds to another's. Clouds of mosquitos from the surrounding jungle bedeviled the wounded and sound alike. The insects carried parasites that caused malaria, and, on the anopheles-infested peninsula of Bataan, there was no quinine. Men dropped like flies, sweating and moaning in delirium, as the disease burst from their livers and into their bloodstreams. The Japanese Zeros relentlessly ripped the jungle canopy overhead— the men's only shelter—into shreds with their bombs.[4] The sun beat down with a flattening heat, more than ninety degrees Fahrenheit and 100 percent humidity.[5] Hope dripped away like rancid sweat.

Still the troops fought on. Firing machine guns held together with parts cobbled from crashed airplanes and using rusty weapons left over from WWI, they battled as they could.[6] Sailors became infantrymen and soldiers became medics, carrying the wounded on their backs since there were no ambulances or litters for transport. The sick lay trembling in ditches as the earth shook around them.

No help was forthcoming. MacArthur's War Plan Orange decreed that Manila be declared an "Open City," an attempt to avoid further devastation that did little to stop the Japanese from flattening the city regardless. The outgunned Americans and Filipino Army Scouts had withdrawn from the capital, heading to the Bataan Peninsula to have one last stand-off with Japan's invading Imperial Army.

Bataan had been chosen as the "perfect" defensive position. Perfect, that is, if the US Army had only to hold that position long enough for the US Navy to steam across the Pacific, like the cavalry of old, with reinforcements and resupplies. The flaw in the plan was obvious. After Pearl Harbor, there *was* no US Navy to ride to the rescue, and with no air cover, the troops were hopelessly exposed.

By year's end, the War Department in Washington had come to regard the Philippines as a lost cause. President Roosevelt had decided to use American resources in the European theater rather than try to wage a war on two fronts. War Secretary Stimson had even said to Winston Churchill, "There are times men have to die."[7]

That didn't stop Roosevelt's relentless propaganda machine from broadcasting the President's message to the Filipino people on December 28, 1941, in which he said, "I give to the people of the Philippines my solemn pledge that their freedom will be redeemed and their independence established and protected. The entire resources in men and materials of the United States stand behind that pledge.... The United States Navy is following an intensive and well-planned campaign against Japanese forces, which will result in positive assistance to the defense of the Philippine Islands."[8]

The president even assured MacArthur, who showed remarkable gullibility, that "every ship at our disposal is bringing to the South West Pacific the forces which will ultimately smash the invader."[9]

MacArthur chose to swallow this fabrication whole cloth, and on January 15, 1942, sent a missive to the troops still battling on Bataan:

"Thousands of troops and hundreds of planes are being dispatched. The exact time and arrival of reinforcements is unknown, and they will have to fight their way through Japanese attempts against them. It is imperative that our troops hold until their reinforcements arrive. No further retreat is possible. Our supplies are ample; a determined defense will defeat the enemy's attack. It is a question now of courage and determination. Men who run will merely be destroyed, but men who fight will save themselves and their country. I call upon every soldier in Bataan to fight in his assigned position, resisting every attack."[10]

The troops—sick, starving, and abandoned—knew better.

War correspondent Frank Hewett gave voice to the despair running through the ranks and forever dubbed the troops "The Battling Bastards of Bataan":

No mama, no papa, no Uncle Sam,
No aunts, no uncles, no cousins, no nieces,
No pills, no planes, no artillery pieces,
And nobody gives a damn![11]

Henry G. Lee was a twenty-seven-year-old recruit and amateur poet, serving with the Philippine Division of the US forces, who kept a journal throughout those endless days and nights during the defense of Bataan. One of his poems speaks of the inexplicable drive that kept the men going when death often seemed it might be a relief:

I see no gleam of victory alluring
No chance of splendid booty or of gain
If I endure—I must go on enduring
And my reward for bearing pain—is pain
Yet, though the thrill, the zest, the hope are gone
Something within me keeps me fighting on."[12]

They fought until they could fight no more. On April 9, 1942, the US forces laid down their arms in what would prove to be a surrender larger than any other in American history *except* for the surrender of the Confederate Army at Appomattox, an event that took place on exactly that date seventy-seven years before during the Civil War.

Approximately seventy-six thousand American and Filipino soldiers had been fighting on Bataan, and Maj. Gen. Edward King, commanding officer and a zealous student of the Civil War, remarked that he knew how Gen. Robert E. Lee had felt when he said about surrendering to General Grant, "I would rather die a thousand deaths."[13]

ACROSS THE BAY at Corregidor, Minter and the rest of his troops were in somewhat better shape, but prospects were not particularly good. On April 9, 1942, he wrote a short letter to Lisa. It read, "I am enclosing postal insurance receipt for xmas presents on which you might be able to collect in case they didn't arrive."

Canopy cover had been stripped after all the strafing runs by the Japanese. Bomb craters served as natural foxholes, augmenting the tunnels with which the defending troops had honeycombed the island. Minter remained at his post in the relative safety of the operations bunker in the Malinta Tunnel. But life in the tunnel was far from agreeable, being rocked by bombs incessantly, with the men living in poorly illuminated, filthy, and cramped quarters.

Despite having vowed to "share the fate of my men," MacArthur left the area in March on a boat bound for Australia. He took with him his family and several officers. Family legend has it that Minter's mother hounded her DC neighbor Arthur MacArthur, General MacArthur's brother, to ensure Minter was offered a seat on that escape boat. Minter, however, turned it down to stay with his men. He became, like all of the men left behind, a target.

Once Bataan had fallen, the Japanese turned their full attention to Corregidor, a seemingly impregnable fortress known as "The Rock." Guarding Manila Bay, the finest natural harbor in Asia, Corregidor was equipped with twenty-three batteries, many predating WWI. The biggest were Batteries Hearn and Smith, with impressive twelve-inch west-ranging guns that were capable of firing a thousand-pound shell with a maximum range of twenty-nine thousand yards (about twenty-seven kilometers).[14]

Japan needed to control Corregidor so that their ships had free passage in and out of Manila Bay. To accomplish that, Lt. Gen. Masaharu Homma ordered his big guns sighted on the tadpole-shaped island in preparation for an amphibious assault. To mount those guns properly, however, the seventy-six thousand American and Filipino soldiers captured on Bataan had to be moved out of the way, and quickly.[15]

These prisoners of war (POWs) were to be moved to San Fernando Pampanga, located seventy-five miles north of Bataan's tip.

They were then to be carted by rail in boxcars up to Capas, before marching the final eight miles to Camp O'Donnell, a former Filipino training installation. Virtually all prisoners—including officers—were expected to go by foot to San Fernando. Thus began the infamous Bataan Death March.

The POWs received little food or water, and many died along the way from heat or exhaustion. POWs drank water from filthy water-buffalo wallows on the side of the road. Some Japanese troops, products of a culture that prized order above all, lost control during the chaos that defined the march and beat or bayoneted prisoners who fell behind or were unable to walk. Once the surviving prisoners arrived in Balanga, midway up the peninsula, the overcrowded conditions and poor hygiene caused dysentery and other diseases to spread rapidly. The Japanese failed to provide the prisoners with medical care, leaving a depleted US medical personnel to tend to the sick and wounded (with few or no supplies). Some POWs, however, were luckier. Several hundred actually rode all the way to Camp O'Donnell in trucks.

In a 2001 commemorative speech in front of the US House of Representatives, Rep. Dana Rohrabacher stated:

"They were beaten, and they were starved as they marched. Those who fell were bayoneted. Some of those who were not walking fast enough were beheaded by Japanese officers who were practicing with their samurai swords from horseback. The Japanese culture at that time reflected the view that any warrior who surrendered had no honor; thus, was not fit to be treated like a human being. Thus they were not committing crimes against human beings.... The Japanese soldiers at that time... felt they were dealing with subhumans and animals."[16]

Such an attitude was underscored by the Japanese "Code of Battlefield Conduct" (*Senjinkun*), issued in 1941, which did not cite specific or rigid guidelines to describe how a warrior should behave, nor did it discuss behavior toward enemy combatants. However, it did emphasize that one who allows himself to become a POW has lost all honor.

This was a distortion of a set of attributes used by samurai in Feudal Japan known as *bushido*. The most consistent tenets of *bushido* were: obedience to superiors, loyalty, simplicity, self-discipline, and courage. But there was a widely held samurai belief that only a man with no honor would allow himself to be taken as a prisoner by his enemy. In Medieval Japan, when wars were fought between *daimyos*, the samurai warriors who did surrender "were held in contempt, which made it easier for their captors to rationalize cruelty toward them."[17] Those who fought and died on the field of battle were viewed as extremely courageous, demonstrating their sacrifice to their superiors.[18]

The Japanese judged mercy toward captured or surrendered enemy combatants as weakness, and such prisoners, including the sick and the wounded, were routinely beaten and/or killed. They were convinced any leniency could induce the inferior conquered foe to rebel against their Japanese oppressors. Such rigid thinking fit right in with the mental capacity of the soldiers chosen as guards on Bataan. Japanese society was hierarchical and stratified, which placed a great deal of emphasis on the importance of elitism. In turn, their society believed that the enlisted soldier from the lower classes did not have the mental capacity needed for self-restraint, humane, or ethical treatment of the enemy. Nor should they be allowed the choice to weigh right and wrong decisions.[19] At best, the Japanese hierarchy cast a blind eye to cruelty. Mostly, though, they encouraged it and led by example. The guards were gruesome captors, at the lowest end of the totem pole, and, thus, with the biggest chip on their shoulders.

Trucks drove over some of those who fell or succumbed to fatigue. "Cleanup crews" put to death those too weak to continue, though some trucks picked up some of those too fatigued to stay on their feet. Some marchers were harassed with random bayonet stabs and beatings.

Approximately ten thousand American and Filipino prisoners died on the sixty-five-mile march.[20] Had the deaths been apportioned evenly over the entire sixty-five-mile route, one would have encountered a corpse every twenty yards.[21]

Minter, still in the relative safety of Corregidor, attempted to get a letter and a telegram to Lisa for their March anniversary, finally succeeding on April 10. In them, he wrote that, "Life with you has been and will be more wonderful than words can express," and assured her that he was "still going strong." That latter sentiment wasn't true.

The defenders of Corregidor had been bombed since December 28, 1941. Those bombings became incessant on Corregidor once Bataan fell. For several days, the bombing followed a regular pattern. Every four hours of every day, for between fifteen and fifty minutes, Japanese bombers and artillery pelted the island of Corregidor. Conversations had to be stopped, sleep disrupted, and men found breathing the already dank air even harder. Rations were indefinitely cut in half. At midnight, with military precision, the last bombing run of the day took place. As the days dragged on, the US forces were living on only thirty ounces of food a day. Mules that were killed in the shelling were dragged underground and cooked in the makeshift messes.

More than a thousand sick and wounded men were sheltered in the Malinta Tunnel. The defenders above were running out of ammo. The Japanese were not. On May 4 alone, it was estimated that sixteen thousand shells hit the 4.9 square miles of tiny Corregidor. Corregidor had the dubious distinction of being the most-bombed place in the war, along with Malta.[22]

Later one night, sitting on a log inside the tunnel, Minter listened to the men—mostly officers—talk about the Bataan defeat. Word of the march and its conditions came in increasingly exaggerated sound bites. Cobbling together everything he had heard from the various sources, Minter ruminated that there had to have been over a million prisoners for everything to be true. But the misery of the march seemed unfathomable, totally inconceivable.

Such cruelty could not have taken place, Minter thought. We are men, not savages.

Just then, the log on which Minter was seated began to shake. At first, he half expected there to be the sound of crashing bombs, as he had so often heard before. The shaking continued and got heavier. It seemed to spread to the floor.

"It's an earthquake!" someone shouted.

No one moved.

Someone else shouted out, "The Japs have stooped so low that if they don't get us with bombs, they'll order up an earthquake."

The men laughed nervously. The rumbling finally subsided, the only remnant of the shaking a steady stream of dust falling from the cave's roof.

Yet, much to the embarrassment of the Japanese, the defending troops fought on. During the final days of the battle, Minter was not among them. He had succumbed to pneumonia and was bedridden and next to death, having dropped to below 165 pounds from his usual 190. On May 5, his convalescence was interrupted. The Japanese forces led by Maj. Gen. Kureo Taniguchi boarded landing craft and barges and headed for the final assault on Corregidor.

On May 3, Minter sent a remarkably upbeat and rather untrue letter to his anxious wife:

> ... It looks as though the general picture of our war effort is improving.... I am in splendid health.... Remember that I worship you and always will.

After fierce resistance and mindful of the thousand incapacitated men in the tunnel, American Lt. Gen. Jonathan Wainwright radioed President Roosevelt on May 6:

> "There is a limit of human endurance, and that point has long been passed. With broken heart and head bowed in sadness, but

not shame, I must arrange terms for the surrender of the fortified Islands of Manila Bay."[23]

After burning the national colors to prevent their capture by
the enemy, Wainwright sent two officers with a white flag to the
Japanese. Corregidor had been surrendered.

Of the approximately twelve thousand surviving members of
the military, there were about fifteen hundred US Marines and
eight thousand Army (US and Filipino) members; the rest were
Navy personnel. All were taken as prisoners of war. Captain
Hoeffel, the highest-ranking naval officer on Corregidor, sent the
following message over the Navy transmitters before he joined
his men in line: "One hundred seventy three officers and two
thousand three hundred and seventeen enlisted men of the Navy
reaffirm their loyalty and devotion to country, family, and friends."
This number included the ranks of Navy personnel from all the
fortified islands in Manila Bay. There was no indication of casualties. But, with word of the Bataan treatment, imprisonment was
no safe harbor.

Captain Hoeffel would later report to the family that Minter
had been very ill during the surrender and had to be carried out
by stretcher.

ON MAY 9, Lisa received the cable she had been dreading:

Washington Govt. to Mrs. N. Minter Dial
      The Navy Department exceedingly regrets to advise you
that, according to the records of this department, your husband,
Nathaniel Minter Dial, United State Navy, was performing his
duty in the service of his country in the Manila Bay area, when
that station capitulated. He will be carried on the records of the
Navy Department as Missing pending further information. No
report of his death or injury has been received and he may be a
Prisoner of War....

The next day, through her unending tears, Lisa read a newly received letter sent by Minter's friend, Navy Lt. Bob Taylor, who was stationed in Papua, New Guinea. In the letter, Taylor passed along information he received from another Navy man, Bernard "Brute" Roeder. Roeder had escaped from Corregidor with the help of a guerrilla band that arranged a small boat in which Roeder sailed to the southern islands of the Philippines and from there to New Guinea. Taylor tried to put a good spin on the bad news:

... Please remember that a prisoner of war has some advantages. Minter isn't fighting anymore, and he is fed more than the poor devils on Corregidor have been getting.

With a horrific sense of *déjà vu*, Lisa read his next words:

I know you will continue to be a brave girl about the whole thing. Chin up, Lisa.

To say Minter was one of the lucky ones was to speak in relative terms. The lucky ones were the guys who had escaped after Corregidor fell—running through the jungle, heading for a boat, or anything that could pass for a boat, before they had to face capture by the Japanese.

But, Minter was lucky in that he was spared the infamous Bataan Death March, where so many men suffered the ignominy of being killed as a prisoner.

When Corregidor surrendered, Minter was so ill with pneumonia that, after being carried out of the tunnel where he and the rest of the US command on the Rock had been sheltering, the Japanese had initially left him behind. They herded most of the rest of the captured troops like cattle—driving the starving men before them with swords, bayonets, and cudgels. Many men died within hours.

For the first seven days of captivity, the prisoners were kept in a concrete yard (called, ironically, the Kindley Field or the 92nd

Garage, as it had been the motor pool for the 92nd Coastal Artillery) without shelter or food and with only one spigot as the source of water for everyone. It took twelve hours in line for any man to fill his canteen—if he still had one to fill. The prisoners were kept in these torrid conditions with no sanitation until May 23, when they were barged to Manila and paraded down Dewey Boulevard as spoils of Japanese victory.

Sometime in June, Minter was sent north to the soon-to-be notorious Cabanatuan Prison Camps Nos. 1 and 3 (in central Luzon). He had, it was reported, recovered from his pneumonia, but the situation in the camps was not fit for sick men.[24] Conditions, especially in the first few months of captivity, were unfathomably bad. Minter got dysentery, as almost all his fellow prisoners did. Tropical diseases spread through the ranks of the weakened and starving men like wildfire. Simple cuts or wounds frequently brought on serious infections and, sometimes, gangrene. The makeshift hospital ward was overflowing. Men deemed to be in their final stages were sent to Zero Ward.

The prisoners had been moved to open-ended longhouses, with only rudimentary walls, thatched *nipa* roofs, and dirt floors. At first, it appeared as though the Japanese might honor the unwritten rules of war, which said officers should be accorded a better level of treatment than enlisted men, but that was soon shown to be a fallacy. Officers were kept separately from those of lower ranks in their own thatched enclosure, but the better level of treatment didn't exist.

Whistleseed soup and *lugao*, a blue-tinted watery rice, often crunchy with maggots, was the only food distributed, and only at random times. Water was supplied in one dirty bucket per building and another bucket served as the head, to be shared evenly with the poor wretches who couldn't quite make it to the bucket because of dysentery. Mucus and blood-filled diarrhea, the most classic symptom of the disease, spattered the floor. There was no water to clean up the mess. The men used ripped pieces of their uniforms as rags and kicked dirt over the rest. The stench, exacerbated by the summer heat, well into the nineties, soon became unbearable, and with the stink came even more hordes of biting flies—black flies, green blowflies, bluebottle flies—and mosquitos.

Rickety and putrid double-decker sleeping bays smelled of sweat, gangrenous wounds, and death. Bedbugs and lice became everyone's constant companions.

Even the few men able to stay relatively healthy couldn't sleep and were driven to near madness by the terrible trio of exhaustion, heat, and thirst. Going without food made men weak. Going without water made them insane. Some howled all night. Others ran out of the hovels shrieking, only to be bayoneted or beheaded by guards trying to save bullets. Everyone dreamed of escape.

In the beginning, the prisoners were given nothing to do, and indolence proved one of the greatest torments of all. Soon, though, grave-digging became a shared occupation. The men were allowed to bury the dead, and anyone who was strong enough volunteered to help do so. As the prisoners grew weaker, the burials became more cursory, and a limb or hand left exposed would be eaten by wild dogs at night.

Keeping up with the dead became a full-time occupation, as the death rate at Cabanatuan during the first few months was astounding. In June 1942, there were 487 deaths. In July, 801 men were buried—more than twenty-six per day. In August, the figures showed that some control had been established, with the loss of 287 men. September counted 256; October, 248; November, 296; December, 136. By April 1943, the death rate had slowed down to the single digits, if only because of the lower number of living men available to die. At the Memorial Day service on May 30, 1944, prayers were said for the 2,645 buried Americans.[25] The dead were stacked behind the barracks like cordwood, and, as the monsoon season came, hastily dug graves filled with water and often floated the corpses out of the ground.

Minter eventually recovered from his pneumonia and, as one of the tallest and sturdiest men among the prisoners, would find his height and breadth both a blessing and a curse. He could help with the hardest work, like digging the graves—sparing weaker men—and his relative strength earned him a coveted spot on the "wood detail" when jobs were finally assigned by the guards.

The wood-chopping detail meant getting up with the sun, walking a distance of about five miles, cutting wood, and then carrying back logs, averaging four to six feet long six to eight inches in diameter. The men on this detail couldn't be too sickly and got a slightly bigger ration of rice to be able to continue such manual labor. Another advantage was that the guards were less attentive on that detail, and the prisoners could hide eggs given to them by sympathetic Filipinos they encountered in the fields, in holes hand-carved into the bottoms of their canteens.[26]

But the Japanese had an inferiority complex about their usual diminutive stature as opposed to the taller Americans. They didn't like looking up at the prisoners. Someone like Minter no doubt experienced what happened when a shorter, rage-filled guard held total power over a prisoner of more than six feet in height.

John Oleksa, a fellow prisoner and former cook on the *Napa*, remembered, "The Japs always picked on the real tall guys because, you know, they felt so inferior to them.... Something they liked to do was to use the tools with which they were working, like a shovel or a pick, and they made [the prisoner] put it under the arm or behind the legs, until the circulation got cut off. Then the person would fall over, and they would start kicking him."[27]

Kicking was the least of the physical torture of prisoners. Anyone possessing anything that read "Made in Japan" was likely to be bayoneted for disrespect to the Empire. If having their entrails removed didn't kill them, the men were left to die and bloat in the heat where they fell. Men seen with rings like Minter's Annapolis class ring might have the finger or even an entire hand cut off in order for the captor to claim the trophy. Guards swung swords indiscriminately from trucks passing work details on the roads, and prisoners were randomly beheaded.

Faced with such inhuman treatment, the prisoners of Cabanatuan obsessively plotted escape. A few of them got free, making their way by hook or by crook to Australia or other destinations in the south to reunite with their company. These are the men who lived to tell the tales of what went on to the survivors of Bataan and Corregidor. Others failed in their escape attempts, and the punishment was sadistic if not always fatal.

In one instance, an attempt to escape was made by two Army officers and an officer in the Navy's Civil Engineer Corps. On a very dark night, the men tried to leave by crawling along a ditch to get around the razor wire bordering the camp. They had almost made it, when an Army-enlisted man stumbled over them and made some noise. Propelled by adrenaline and fear, the escapees sprang out of the ditch to pummel the Army man. Other prisoners joined in the fracas, and things got rowdy enough to draw the attention of the guards who heard the English word "escape" and dragged the three escapees out of the ditch. They were beaten on their feet and legs until they were unable to stand. When they fell, the guards jumped up and down on their ribs and abdomens. Left out all night, bleeding and lying in their own vomit, the men were marched out in the morning to the main road, where they were in full view of the camp. Their hands were bound behind them and tied to a beam overhead so they were forced to remain standing. They were then beaten with clubs and boards. Any Filipino who passed by on the road was forced to strike the men in the face with a club supplied by the guards. If the blow wasn't deemed hard enough, the Filipino was beaten also.

Blood encircled the bound men's feet. They hung there for two full days, a sight most of their fellow prisoners couldn't endure. They turned away, shuffling back into their barracks with hatred in their hearts.

On the third day, a typhoon struck and the tortured men were hit with debris propelled by hurricane-force winds. When the weather cleared, it was revealed the men were still alive, though so battered as to be unrecognizable. One man's ear had been torn off and was lying on his shoulder.

Their groans and screams, delivered through broken jaws and teeth, could be heard throughout the camp. The other prisoners knew it was a blessing when the guards finally cut them down and took them for execution. Two were shot and the third beheaded.[28]

To thwart further attempts to escape, the Japanese grouped the prisoners into bands of ten, or "Death Squads." If one of the group should try to escape, the remaining nine would be killed in retribution. This put an end to escape attempts.

Attempting escape was not the only transgression that would bring the wrath of the guards down on the prisoners' heads. Trying to find food was another.

One of those who made good his escape to Australia, Lt. Col. S.M. Mellnik, related this horrific tale after the war:

"Five enlisted men were arrested by the Japs on the charge that they had been dealing through the fence with friendly Filipinos. Two of these Filipinos were also caught, and all seven of the men freely admitted their guilt, pointing out that their only crime was an attempt to get more food.

As punishment, all seven men were tied up to stakes just outside the camp and allowed no food or water for forty-eight hours. In tying one of the Americans, the Japanese guards bungled the job, and this man finally freed his hands from the bonds that bound them.

At noon on the second day, as the temperature soared near one hundred degrees and the sun beat down directly overhead, this enlisted man, crazed by the combination of heat, hunger, and thirst, jerked himself free, ran for the stockade gate, and let himself back into the prison. Once inside his own barracks, he fell on his knees at the water bucket, drank like a man possessed, and collapsed onto his bunk.

Despite the fact that this prisoner voluntarily ran back inside the prison stockade, the Japs made a great commotion over their charge of attempted escape. At about five o'clock that afternoon, all prisoners were herded into our barracks under guard. Nonetheless, through the chinks of the flimsy walls, they all stood witness to what happened next. All seven men were summarily shot to death. Again, there was no trial."[29]

DURING THE EARLY stages of captivity, Ken Wheeler, who had also been stationed in the 16th Naval District, became good friends with Minter. They met at the time of the surrender and wound up in the same barracks. Wheeler said of Minter, "He handled himself so well in those first days. He, among all the others, was one of the few who stood very straight. He was a strong man, with guts. Being a little older, he became a leader among the men. He always conducted himself well. He did it right."[30]

One of the ways Minter tried to ease the burden of his fellow prisoners was by reading aloud to them at night from the limited library the men had scrounged together. In doing so, he must have recollected when he, Lisa, and Ruffin had done the same on those evenings back in California. It would have seemed another lifetime. Minter read Stephen Vincent Benét and Frank Desprez's works so often, he'd memorized them.

Lt. (junior grade) Meade H. Willis Jr. was another of Minter's barracks mates. Willis kept a diary he managed to hide from his captors and which he used to write his memoirs after the war. He remembered Minter fondly in its pages, while glossing over the indescribable conditions:

> "We have been put into a barracks in the lowest part of the camp, which turns out to be the worst location. Turk, Sanborn, and Berry escaped (successfully for about two months). We were moved to Barracks 21 for a while and then to Barracks 2 for our permanent home. Lloyd Wagner was our Barracks leader and does a damn good job.... We have much freedom in camp, and

were it not for the filthy heads, flies, mosquitoes, and disease, life wouldn't be so bad....We are pretty lucky because our barracks group is congenial, everyone keeping themselves in fair shape. I swelled up pretty bad at one time and had tropical ulcers but nothing serious. Jim Crotty, Harry Morton and Fred Hazan died. I enjoyed Warwick Scott a lot. He is an extremely interesting man, very intellectual and ambitious and a perfect gentleman... firm and convincing in his views. Malcolm Douglas [Minter's usher], Shofner, Minter Dial, Ken Wheeler, Whit Cook and Al Moffett were others I liked."31

Captivity made strong allegiances, but it is one of the ironies of Minter's story that fellow barracks-mate Lt. Warwick Scott was the uncle of the girl whom Minter's son, Victor, would eventually marry—my mother, Alexandra Montgomery.

Some old ties had to be broken. Machinist Mate 2nd class Harry L. Richardson, one of the crewmen from the *Napa* of which Minter was captain, was about to be transferred to mainland Japan in July of 1943. He made a point of seeking out his old skipper first.

"The last time I saw the 'Boss' was in Cabanatuan number one before I left for Japan on the twenty-third of July. No tears or anything like that, just a good handshake, hoping to see each other again stateside. He was always conscious about his men. He told me to 'keep my powder dry' as we used to say."32

Richardson had tried to stay in contact with *Napa* crewmembers and officers, specifically Minter, since leaving the ship back in March 1942. Neither of the two other *Napa* officers—men with whom Minter would most likely have stayed in contact when conditions permitted—survived the war.

Officers were generally older men, and the camp was no respecter of age. For a brief time, there were three thousand officers at Cabanatuan—however, many succumbed to illness or torture or volunteered to be sent to Japanese work camps hoping to find less horrendous conditions.

In some cases the officers bore the brunt of the aggression, being made to serve as examples to the rest of the prisoners. Captain Adair (US Army) wrote, "I might sound prejudiced, having been an officer; but I believe that they treated us worse, because it was the Japanese-enlisted men that we came into contact with, and they took advantage of their position and pushed the officers around a little more."[33]

Many of the men on the Bataan Death March had ended up at Camp O'Donnell, a place at which "Americans had not seen deprivational grotesqueries on such a vast scale since the days of Andersonville, the infamous Civil War death camp," wrote historian Hampton Sides.

For his part, one prisoner wrote, "Hell is only a state of mind; O'Donnell was a place."[34]

Capt. Austin C. Shofner had been a prisoner at both Cabanatuan and Camp O'Donnell. "When it came to sadism, cruelty, and barbaric punishments, Cabanatuan far exceeded O'Donnell," he swore.[35]

By their unrelenting sadistic acts, the guards at Cabanatuan earned their nicknames: The Body Snatcher, Blood, The Maggot, Frankenstein, Bloodhound, Slime—and yet, in their limited communications, Minter and his fellow prisoners never let on what they were living through to their loved ones back home.[36]

Lies of omission were acts of love.

BACK AT HOME, four-year-old Victor was running proudly around the house with a Navy Cross medal pinned to his chest, saying to his mother, "Try and be brave, just like my daddy." The medal was sent to Lisa in the autumn of 1942, its official citation reading:

"For heroism in combat with the enemy during the period December 7, 1941, to March 18, 1942, as Commanding Officer of the USS *Napa*. While exposed to frequent horizontal and dive bombing attacks by enemy Japanese air forces, Lieutenant Dial directed the anti-aircraft batteries of his ship and conducted operations of strategic importance involving hazardous missions such as to bring great credit to his command and the United States Naval Service."

Minter was a hero, or so said the United States government when he was awarded the prestigious Navy Cross, an honor awarded only to a very few.[37]

The most specific act of his heroism involved boarding a supply-laden merchant vessel that had been abandoned by its crew under fire. He then sailed it into Cavite under a rain of Japanese bombs, bringing the supplies safely back to headquarters.[38]

The honor was cold comfort to Lisa. Her pride in Minter did not quell the rising hysteria she felt. Yet she kept up appearances, knowing Minter would want her to do so. She even gritted her teeth and gave a smiling interview to a local journalist.

The Press Telegram and Long Beach Sun, May 5, 1942
WIFE HEARS HUSBAND ON CORREGIDOR
"... Expressing happiness over her husband's safety, Mrs. Dial said that only a woman in a like position can know what it really means to have one's husband and the children's 'daddy' safe in the midst of terrifying and destructive elements. His bravery, she asserts, is a part of his duties as an officer of the US Navy...."[39]

Lisa hung on every unremittingly cheerful word about Minter written by his comrades in letters to her. This letter from Lt. Rufus Taylor was delivered via Coronado, California, on December 6, 1942:

June 12, 1942
My dear Lisa,
    In all likelihood, you'll not remember me so I'll explain that I served with Minter on the Arizona in 1934 and 1935 and there

formed a liking and regard for him that has increased with each contact in subsequent years.

I last saw Minter at Corregidor in April. He was serving as aide to the Commandant to which job he had been assigned after his ship was destroyed. He was quite sound and well and consistently cheerful performing his duties with his usual quiet efficiency without regard to the unfortunate circumstances in which all there were placed. His position as aide to the Commandant, who stuck to his post until the surrender, made it necessary for Minter to remain also. Knowing the circumstances rather well, I presume Minter was made prisoner of war.

... We have every reason to believe and hope he will be returned to you safe and sound when this war is over and in the meantime you have much more reason to be proud of your husband who upholds all the best traditions of the Service and who has the best professional respect as well as the warm personal affection of all of us who have had the good fortune to serve with or near him.

Most sincerely and sympathetically,

Rufus L. Taylor

From Lt. Cdr. Bill H. Kirvan, the letter below was written while aboard the USS *Temptress*:

June 13, 1942

Dear Lisa,

I recently arrived in port and confirmed what I have feared since the fall of Corregidor—that Minter is missing. I fully realize the futility of words at a time like this and I further realize that each day of waiting and hoping must be an agonizing ordeal in itself that can be borne only by you.

But I do want to express on behalf of Ruth and myself, our most heartfelt sympathy and to assure you that we, like the

remainder of your... friends, are praying that Minter will be
returned safely to you, Diana and Vicky.

It may be that you have heard already that Minter is safe and
well. However, if you haven't, "keep your chin up" with the real-
ization that communications are extremely slow these days....

Sincerely,

Bill

And from Brute Roeder, who had been stationed with Minter
in the Philippines and had made good his escape:

July 30, 1942

Dear Lisa,

... We have had some luck out here, but the Asiatic fleet did
a magnificent job with meager resources at hand and upheld
the finest traditions of the Navy. I have questioned each officer
and man who have come down [from the Philippines] and they
all said that Minter was in good health and were unanimous in
their praise of his hard and important work. You must be very
proud of him....

Sincerely,

Brute Roeder

Minter's mother was fiercely proud of her son and said as much
to the press at every opportunity. Using her contacts as a former
senator's wife, Jou-Jou kept Minter's name in the papers as though
the very appearance of his name could somehow keep him alive
in the hell of Cabanatuan. Newspapers like the *Washington Post*
ran stories touting Minter's bravery and valor. Local papers back
home in South Carolina made much of their homegrown hero:

The Greenville Daily, South Carolina, April 11, 1942

LIEUTENANT DIAL ON CORREGIDOR, MOTHER IS TOLD

Former Laurens Resident Has Escaped Death in Bataan Fighting

ANNAPOLIS GRADUATE

Mrs. Nathaniel B. Dial, formerly of Laurens, SC, widow of the late South Carolina senator, and mother of Lieut. NM Dial, said today that the latest word she had received in regard to the safety of her son was that he reached Corregidor.

Lieut. Dial has been in the thick of the fight to hold Bataan for four months, his mother said. He was in command of the USS *Napa*, an 845-ton tug operating in Manila.

Mrs. Dial said that until last week she had had no word from her son in the last four months. She received three letters last week and on Monday of this week she received a cablegram stating that he was safe.

IN TOUGH SPOT

"I realize he is in a tough spot." she said, "but I have a strong feeling that he will come out all right. I am so thankful that he has come through the four-month-long struggle in Bataan."

Lieut. Dial's ship, the USS *Napa*, the submarine tender *Canopus*, the minesweeper *Bittern*, and the 500-foot dry dock *Dewey*, were ordered destroyed by Capt. Kenneth M. Hoeffel, in charge of land fighting sailors, to render the ships useless to the enemy, the Navy department revealed today.

Lieutenant Dial, 31 years old last month, is married and has two children, who are with their mother at their Long Beach, California, home.[40]

Both Lisa and Jou-Jou sent letters regularly. Until November of 1943, however, when the Japanese finally released all of the prisoners' mail at once, Minter had received none of them. We now know Minter got a total of six letters from Lisa (one with photos of her and the children) and two from his mother during his captivity. After May of 1944, no more letters were delivered.[41]

But Lisa kept on writing. One particularly plaintive letter survives (having been sent back, undelivered):

Friday, July 24, 1942

My dearest love,

A year ago tonight we were en route to the West Coast. I don't remember the town we spent the night in though, do you?

We were trying so hard to be brave—and how little we knew of what was ahead of us then. I'm glad we didn't—I never would have let you go—I couldn't ever have said good-bye.

Now we have to try so much harder to be brave, but you'd be proud of us, if you could see us darling....

Last night I had the greatest thrill I could possibly have except seeing you—I talked with a Com. (I don't dare mention names in this letter) but he slept in the bunk below you at Corregidor! He and his wife came to see me—and he told me all he could about you! Oh you can't imagine what it did to me! It was terrific! I was greatly comforted by all he said, though he may have exaggerated the good things to lessen the bad, but still I feel encouraged.

And oh, that feeling of knowing that someday you will come home to me is so tremendous—so overpowering—that I can't be gotten down. He and another Com. that got out with him are both going back to sea in a few days so their battles, or strains, are not over yet, and yours are.

Oh dearest, feel my calmness and my faith. I know life isn't pleasant where you are, but it is life. Keep remembering us and our whole long future together.

Write often to me—that helps, I know it does. Because I always feel closer to you when I'm writing to you. You won't have activities you can tell me—but you must tell me your thoughts—and your dreams and your hopes—everything....

Oh dearest, I feel so terribly much that I can't express. I don't even know that my letters will ever reach you. But that means that we must stay all the closer in our hearts. Look toward the sea tonight and call my name. I'll hear you dearest—I'll hear you—and I'll answer with a kiss. The breeze will brush it against your lips—from me. Don't ever lose hope, darling. Live for our future.

    I'll adore you forever,

      Lisa.

Minter never read the letter. It was returned with a note:

"This communication is returned to sender because the addressee has not been officially listed as a prisoner of war. Immediately upon receipt of official information from the enemy power holding prisoners, the Information Branch Aliens Division, Provost Marshal General's Office, Washington, D.C. informs the next of kin of the correct mailing address. No attempt should be made to correspond with anyone through prisoner of war correspondence channels until that person has been officially designated as a Prisoner of War by the appropriate Military or Naval authority."

Downhearted, but not extinguished, Lisa tried sending wires, like this one late in 1942:

DEAREST, EVERYBODY WELL. VIC, DIANA KINDERGARTEN LOVING YOU DEARLY. BE BRAVE, LIVE FOR FUTURE. ANSWER YOUR HEALTH AND CONDITIONS IF POSSIBLE. GOD BLESS YOU. LISA.

The silence was deafening, broken only by news occasionally received from men returning from the area, via letters with news transmitted on illegal radios, or via escaped prisoners.

In the service agenda pamphlet printed by the Washington Heights Presbyterian Church for the Sunday, August 22, 1943, service, it read under personals:

"A letter lately received from Maj. Gen. Rush B. Lincoln brought cheering news of his own safety in New Caledonia, and as well most welcome word through an escaped prisoner of a Jap camp near Manila that he had recently seen Lt. Commander Minter Dial concerning whom we have so long and anxiously awaited news. He reported Minter alive and as well as could be expected."

There was also a shortwave message from Japan, intercepted January 5, 1944, 8:40 a.m., that said:

"This is Meade H. Willis Junior broadcasting through radio Tokyo from Zentsuji War Prison Camp, Shikoku Japan, to Mr. and Mrs. Meade H Willis at Winston-Salem, North Carolina:

Hello Mother and Dad. Hope everyone is well and that everything is all right. For goodness sakes, don't worry about me. I'm in good health and spirits considering I was captured on Corregidor May 6, 1942.

... Douglas Fisher, 490 Jerry Street, San Francisco, California; Minter Dial, Laurens, South Carolina, friends of mine there [are okay in the Philippines].

... Tell everyone in the bank hello. I am studying and reading and lecturing a little on banking and related subjects.... I am growing a beard that would make Stonewall Jackson turn over in his grave...."[42]

Maj. Michiel Dobervich, who was a friend of Minter's, was one of the prisoners who had escaped. Lisa received two letters from him, filled with incorrect but optimistic references to prisoners' mail being received and camp conditions improving.

Major US Marine Corps Fargo, North Dakota
February 2, 1944
Dear Mrs. Dial,

I know Lt. Nathaniel Dial. He was in excellent health and spirits. He is now in Camp No. 1 located at Cabanatuan on the island of Luzon. I last saw him October 26, 1942. They have received Red Cross mail and packages and probably will continue to receive them. Camp conditions have improved over a long period of time and I think they will continue to improve. May God grant his safe return soon.

Sincerely yours,

Major Dobervich.

Major US Marine Corps Falls Church, Virginia

. . .

March 9, 1944

Dear Mrs. Dial,

Minter had received Red Cross Packages, but I do not know whether he had received any mail. In my opinion, he probably has received mail by now, and also more Red Cross packages.

The first two cards sent out by the prisoners were written on or about February and March, 1943. Those were the first two cards you received. The information that he conveyed on those cards is of his own making, and the cards were checked and signed by him so they are authentic. I was in prison long enough to send two of them myself.

Please do not give up hope, and may God grant his safe return soon.

Sincerely,

Michiel Dobervich

The "cards" Dobervich referred to were distributed by the Red Cross to all prisoners of war. Essentially form letters, they contained printed sentences that prisoners could cross out or underline indicating their meaning. Heavily censored, there was a very limited area for prisoners to add personal notes to their loved ones.

Cabanatuan prisoners were also allowed to write four 50-word messages home during a brief span in 1943.[43] Each prisoner was afforded one such card every three months. Delivery was postponed until the censorship had been completed on every one of the prisoners' notes.

In all the messages that were received from Minter, the parts that he filled in appear in **bold** type.

The front of each card was always the same:

SERVICE des PRISONNIERS de GUERRE

Name **NATHANIEL MINTER DIAL**

Nationality **AMERICAN**

Rank **LIEUTENANT NAVY**

Philippine Military Prison Camp **No. 1**

To: **Mrs. N. Minter Dial**

325 Claremont Avenue Long Beach, California

Then, on the back, the messages varied slightly, but were largely boilerplate text with only room for a few words from the prisoner himself.

A document declassified in 2004 on the communications in and out of the Japanese POW camps reported that over the period from August 1943 to August 1944, a total of 23,915 pieces of mail came from the two camps in Cabanatuan, where "about thirty-five hundred POW" had been detained. The report continued, "In the last mail, letters from the Cabanatuan Camps averaged about one letter per person for the half-year period." Clearly, many prisoners were living in a very discouraged state of mind. To put the responses into context, the messages that were tabulated showed the following (from September 1943 through March 1944):

Camp	Total No. of POWs	No. of cards sent	HEALTH				
			Sick in Hospital	Poor	Fair	Good	Excellent
Cabanatuan	2539	2645	5	0	153	1413	968 [1]

In Cabanatuan No. 1, during that period, there were a total of ninety Navy officers and 303 Navy personnel.

Received late in 1943
IMPERIAL JAPANESE ARMY
I am interned at: the Philippine Military Prison Camp #1
My health is—excellent; good; fair; poor.
I am—uninjured; sick in hospital; under treatment; not under treatment.
I am—improving; not improving; better; well.
Please see that: **hugging Victor and Diana for me** is taken care of.
(Re: Family): **All my love (205 pounds) to you and family.**[44]
Please give my best regards to: **all our friends.**

In other messages, Minter used every one of the allowed fifty words to convey his love for Lisa and his children. In this card, received with no date recorded, Minter had to cross out his own name to slip under the word limit. Within it, he inserted a rather cryptic message:

Sweetheart darling, do you know how much you mean to me? You are my reason for being. I realize more and more that you have delightful characteristics Sally plus strength Mary Lou. You are the stout pillar which will hold our tradition until Dad comes home again. All my love, *Minter*

Ruffin Cox interpreted *"Sally plus strength Mary Lou"* for Lisa. He believed Minter was saying, "Sally forth out into the world with strength, my Love."

Received September 1943
IMPERIAL JAPANESE ARMY
I am interned at: the Philippine Military Prison Camp #1
My health is—excellent; good; fair; poor.
I am—uninjured; sick in hospital; under treatment; not under treatment.

I am—improving; not improving; better; <u>well</u>.
Please see that: **everything** is taken care of.
(Re: Family): **All my love to you and family.**
Please give my best regards to: **everyone.**

. . .

Received November 23, 1943
IMPERIAL JAPANESE ARMY
I am interned at: the Philippine Military Prison Camp #1
My health is—excellent; <u>good</u>; fair; poor.
I am—injured; sick in hospital; under treatment; <u>not under treatment</u>.[45]
I am—improving; not improving; better; <u>well</u>.
Please see that: **our dear family** is taken care of.
(Re: Family): **Received mothers [sic] letter. Write and send pictures—Don't worry.**
Please give my best regards to: **family and friends.**

Ominously, the "uninjured" status from the September note becomes "not under treatment" in the November one. Lisa agonized if this meant Minter was hurt and not being treated. Such small changes became huge worries, which caused her to dissolve into tears for hours.

Received December 11, 1943
IMPERIAL JAPANESE ARMY
I am interned at: the Philippine Military Prison Camp #1
My health is—<u>excellent</u>; good; fair; poor.
I am—<u>uninjured</u>; sick in hospital; under treatment; not under treatment.
I am—improving; not improving; better; <u>well</u>.
Please see that: **Victor, Diana—hug the darlings—and you** is taken care of.
(Re: Family): **Tell Sailor to be Dad until I return.**
Please give my best regards to: **all our friends and family.**

One card carried no date, but was clearly written in 1944, on the tenth anniversary of their marriage:

Received packages, one your signature which thrilled me beyond expression. Will drink tenth anniversary toast with postum. Longing for letter but know you keeping home fires burning and that our future together will have added meaning due separation. Remember I love you and always will.

· · ·

Received May 6, 1944
I am interned at—Philippine Military Prison Camp No. 1.
My health is—<u>excellent</u>; good; fair; poor.
 Lisa Darling: though we are apart you seem near and oh so very dear to me. Received two letters from mother, expect yours daily. Anxious hear everything concerning you and our adorable little ones. Ask them save room in their busy lives for me. I love you more each day.

· · ·

No date 1944
 Miss you beyond expression but am wonderfully content knowing that Victor, Diana, hug the darlings, have your undivided attention and devotion of which if I were there would claim so much. My greatest happiness thinking of you and future together. Received your radiogram. Advise Mother. All my love for always.

· · ·

Received July 15, 1944
 My darling: Hoping for pictures though old ones you and adorable children are great comfort. There are no words to express my thankfulness for those wonder-woven bonds that bind us. We will again sit by our fire and have a julep mixed with a silver spoon. All my love, Minter.

But the letter which would come to mean the most to Lisa arrived just before Christmas in 1943:

IMPERIAL JAPANESE ARMY

I am interned at: the Philippine Military Prison Camp #1.

My health is—excellent; <u>good;</u> fair; poor.

I am—injured; sick in hospital; under treatment; <u>not under treatment</u>.

I am—improving; not improving; better; <u>well</u>.

Please see that: **your health** is taken care of.

(Re: Family): **All my love (210 lbs) to you and children.**

Please give my best regards to: **John B. Body, 356-7 Page St., Garden City, N.Y.**

Lisa had never heard of a John Body; but, hoping for further information about Minter from the man, she sent a letter to that address. Several months later, the letter was returned stamped "No such address." Desperate now for word, Lisa tracked down and telephoned—at great expense—the postmaster of Garden City, New York. Eager to help, the postmaster was sorry to tell her that he had served in the position for several decades and there was no such address. He remembered her letter and had racked his brain and searched his records for anyone by the name of John Body, but couldn't find him. Lisa put the letter away, but continued to puzzle over the message's meaning. It wasn't until Minter and Lisa's dear friend Ruffin Cox returned from duty, that the mystery would be solved.

Ruffin recalled to Lisa the times the three of them had spent reading aloud to each other after dinner during those carefree California nights before the war. He then asked her to find her copy of one of their favorites, *John Brown's Body*, by Stephen Vincent Benét. She did so, and Ruffin pointed out the book had been printed in Garden City, New York.

They opened the book to page 356, and what they read—the words of a young Confederate soldier fighting desperately in dire straits against Yankees during the final stages of the American Civil War—brought tears to their eyes:

"... But, women and children, do not fear,
They'll feed the lions and us, next year.
And, women and children, dry your eyes,
The Southern Gentleman never dies.
He just lives on by his strength of will,
Like a damn ole rooster too tough to kill,
Or a brand-new government dollar-bill,
That you can use for a trousers-patch,
Or lightin' a fire, if you've got a match...
Old folks, young folks, never you care,
The Yanks are here and the Yanks are there,
But no Southern gentleman knows despair.
He just goes on in his usual way,
Eatin' a meal every fifteenth day,
And showin' such skill in his change of base,
That he never gets time to wash his face,
While he fights with a fury you'd seldom find..."

Minter had found a way to tell his wife and beloved friend that he, the Southern Gentleman they knew him to be, was fighting with a fury to stay alive and get back home to them.[46]

— 8 —

VICTOR

O NE DAY A NAVAL officer came to my grandmother's house. I don't remember the date, but it must have been well after the end the war. I think I was seven and a half years old. I didn't know who he was; but he was wearing a uniform just like my godfather Ruffin's, who came often to the house to see my mother and me. The strange man talked alone with my mother for quite some time—my mother told me not to stray because he wanted to talk to me too! I wondered why. I could hear her crying and was worried about her.

I learned later that his name was Commander Fisher. We sat together on the porch, my mother and the officer and me. He asked me if I wanted to be in the Navy when I grew up, and I said I hoped so. He said I'd have to study and work hard if that's what I wanted to do, and asked me how I was doing in school. I told him I was already in third grade! My mother told him that I was the youngest boy in the class. I didn't know if that was a good thing or a bad thing.

Then something really surprising happened. He sat me on his knee and gave me a big hug. He said he had something he wanted to give me. He slipped off his gold-colored wrist watch and told me he wanted me to have it. Oh wow! My mother said it was too generous of him, and I shouldn't accept it, but I didn't think so! I begged her to let me keep it, and my father's friend insisted. Finally my mother agreed, thank goodness. I immediately put it on, but it was much too big. Never mind, it was so grown-up to have a watch. I loved it, and I couldn't wait to show it off at school. My mother cautioned that I'd have to be careful that someone didn't steal it from me or that I didn't lose it. I was hardly listening, I was so excited.

I went to sleep that night still wearing the watch, but in the morning my mother found it in my bed—it'd come off during the night. It was just too big. It was the same story the next night. Finally, my mother said she'd better put it in a safe place for me until I was big enough to wear it, and I tearfully agreed.

Even though it was my prized possession, pretty soon I guess I managed to forget about it. Some months later we moved to New York City and then to Connecticut. Somewhere along the line the watch disappeared, or I lost it, or it just vanished.

THE RED CROSS information that was circulated in the United States was designed to comfort the waiting spouses. Optimistic generalizations that appeared in information circulars distributed to the families were therefore as bland and vague as possible:

Information Circular #10
Prisoners of War Information Bureau Office of the Provost Marshal General
This Bureau receives the names of American Prisoners of War and Civilian Internees reported by the enemy powers...
TREATMENT OF PRISONERS: A number of reports from neutral sources indicates [sic] that American Prisoners of War

and civilian internees are receiving fair treatment considering all the circumstances which accompany war.

HEALTH: Under the terms of the Geneva Convention every prison must have a properly equipped infirmary with adequate medical personnel in attendance. All prisoners must be medically examined at least once a month and any who are seriously ill must be admitted to a hospital for treatment. Current information indicates substantial compliance with this requirement.

PAY: The terms of the Geneva Convention pertaining to Officer's pay have been amended to permit the payment of $20, $30 or $40 a month, dependent upon rank. The balance between the amount and regular pay is allowed to accumulate and will be paid to the prisoner upon release. There is no provision for the payment of pay to enlisted men as prisoners of war, but regular pay is allowed to accumulate and will be paid to them upon release....

The truth of what was happening in Cabanatuan was a lot more shocking. Cabanatuan was closer to an extermination camp, albeit one of extermination by neglect.

Food was increasingly meager. Men were forced to supplement their caloric intake by catching and eating one of the rats crawling everywhere as well as anything that could be scavenged from the dead. Eggs or produce stolen while on farm detail could get everyone in a man's death squad of ten fellow prisoners in trouble, shot, or beheaded if found out.

Basic medicines like quinine and sulfa were withheld. Starvation caused prisoners to lose their hair, voices, and teeth. Men went blind. Their skin fell off in patches. Fed only minimal polished rice (which sloughed off the pericarp—the layer that contained vitamin B9), the prisoners developed wet and dry beriberi, which caused their extremities to swell, and forced them into a weird gait called the "Cabanatuan Shuffle." They lost control of their neck muscles from eating rancid fish heads that oozed a neurotoxin.[1]

On September 24, 1944, the camp was aroused by the noise of planes, dozens of them, streaking overhead. They were Navy Hellcats from Adm. Bull Halsey's aircraft carrier, which was steaming in the Philippine Sea, not far from Leyte Gulf. At the Battle of Leyte, which began October 17, General MacArthur at last fulfilled the promise to return that he had made when he stealthily left on a March night in 1942.

The men of Cabanatuan, Minter included, took great heart from seeing the planes—then and over the next days—and hearing distant bombs they dropped.

"We thought, well, it's going to be over in a week or two," recalled Chaplain Robert Preston Taylor.[2] Rumor mills ran rampant. At different times in captivity, the men had managed to fashion a radio out of the most crude of items. But even news over the radio was coated in propaganda. Optimism was the opiate of survival.

But all that hope was dashed when the Japanese announced that another shipment of 1,600 prisoners was being sent to Japan, to be used as slave labor in shipyards, foundries, mines, factories, and mills and to prevent them from falling into American hands. This continued the Japanese policy of recent weeks, during which they had been systematically siphoning off the camp's population, sending prisoners to Manila to board ships bound for mainland Japan. From a peak of eight thousand men, Cabanatuan now only had two thousand, and the majority of them were scheduled to go. The remainder, fewer than five hundred men, were too sick or invalid to move and would be left behind, as Cabanatuan became a "hospital ward."

Many of the men dreaded the trip, believing that the journey, through waters thick with American submarines and bombers overhead, was akin to a death sentence. Others were glad to take their chances in Japan, as they were thoroughly convinced they would never have lived through Cabanatuan. At least, they reasoned, there would be food in Japan. Minter was among those who would rather have stayed through the nightmare that was Cabanatuan, as he reckoned transfer to Japan would mean an even longer time would pass before he could be reunited with Lisa and his family.

But he had no choice. Not among the sickest—and apparently not part of the men who were able to procure the "hot stool" (infected with amoebic dysentery) that had become a camp cottage industry, thus rendering the patient too sick to travel—Minter was among the men trucked down to Bilibid Prison in Manila in October. He would be held there for two months.[3]

If things had been bad at Cabanatuan, they were worse at Bilibid. Shaped in the form of a star, with a central observation tower, Bilibid prison was sordid and overpopulated. The prisoners were put on a starvation diet, and, with no recourse to forage for any other food, did in fact begin starving.[4] Minter knew he and the others might not survive. A few times, notably November 1 as American bombing runs continued, the prisoners were rousted and told they were leaving, only to be sent back at the last moment as movements by American forces made escape too dangerous. Finally, on December 12, a long streak of good weather ended and clouds in the forecast gave the Japanese what they believed would be the best cover to depart. At 6:30 p.m. *tenko* (roll call), the Japanese gave word that the boat would leave the following morning.[5] Minter took up a pen and scratched out a letter to Lisa on ripped book pages he'd been saving.

Dec. 12, 1944
Old Bilibid Prison
Japanese Prison Camp #3
Manila P.I.
Sweetheart darling,
    This is being written on the eve of leaving the above camp for another one probably in Japan proper. There is much to say but time is limited and I know that the things which are really

important between us (and there are so many wonderful ties) are part of our very beings and need no telling.

I have received six letters from you—including the one in which you acknowledged my "rooster" message.[6] Needless to say that was a thrill. So far I have had only the two small snaps of Victor and Diana. Please send lots and lots of pictures including you, your dear self.

I will leave this here with a friend in hopes that it may be started on its way before I would have an opportunity to mail same. We did so hope to be able to stay here ourselves! But providence has been good to me so far. I have faith that my good fortune will continue. I am really in excellent health – still weigh 165 lbs. and have been on the wood chopping detail for almost two years.

I know "Lasca" by heart and most of your favorite passages from John Brown's Body. I even read the entire book (trying to enunciate as you do) to my whole building! Please read the poem "Love" by Roy Croft. It has meant much to me and expresses (in a minor way—no other person could possibly tell how much I really love you) my feeling for you.

I have purposely not tried to give you any advice in my meager messages. I have utmost confidence in your ability and good judgment. Mother has written me a few facts in ref. to the estate and financial matters. There too I have no advice—except to have all capital invested. The children's health and your own is the prime consideration—no expense should be spared to maintain that. If I have received any raise please feel absolutely free to write the Navy Dept. using this letter (if necessary) as authority requesting an increase in allotment to the limit.

Please write to Mother and keep her posted. I haven't written to her – as we are allowed only one card each time and haven't time to write tonight. She has been grand about writing and as devoted and faithful in her confidence in me and in God's protection as I knew she would be.

RIGHT: Josephine "Jou-Jou" Dial with son Minter, 1912

BELOW: Minter (far right) with siblings (l–r) Fannie, Dotty, and Joseph in front of their DC home, 1922

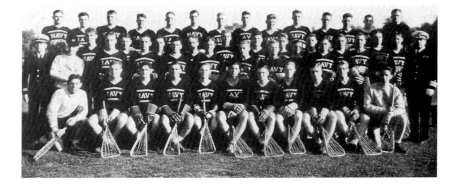

WOODROW WILSON
WASHINGTON D C

20th June 1923

My dear Little Friend,

It is very kind of you to
present me with your first piece of modeling, and
I warmly appreciate it as an evidence of your friendship.
With cordial good wishes,

Sincerely Yours,

Master Minter Dial,
Washington, D. C.

ABOVE, TOP: Young Minter's letter from Woodrow Wilson

ABOVE, BOTTOM: Annapolis Varsity Lacrosse Team, 1932

FACING: Minter with Charlie Keene at Annapolis (courtesy of Sasha Gifford)

CLOCKWISE FROM TOP LEFT: Annapolis 1932 class ring; Minter at his parents' residence, Kalorama Road, Washington, DC; George Washington Pressey at Annapolis (courtesy of Bill Gonyo); Chuck Keene and Minter, mid-1930s (courtesy of Sasha Gifford)

Lisa on her wedding day, March 1934

FACING, CLOCKWISE FROM TOP: Lisa in *Long Beach* magazine;
Minter Dial, c. 1936; Lisa Porter Dial

ABOVE: Minter and Lisa in New York during the World's Fair, 1939

Senator Nathaniel Dial with his grandson, Victor, summer 1940

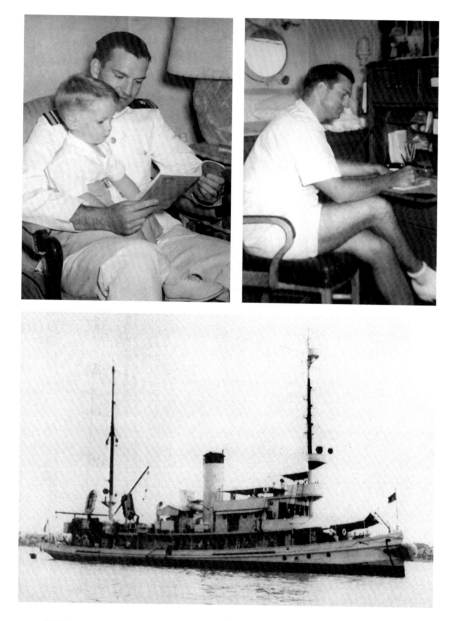

CLOCKWISE FROM TOP LEFT: Lt. Minter Dial with Victor, Christmas 1939; Captain Minter in his cabin, USS *Napa*; Minter's first command, USS *Napa*

TOP: Lisa with Victor and Diana at the end of the war

BOTTOM: Minter at dinner with other officers on board USS *Napa*,
November 1941

THE SECRETARY OF THE NAVY

WASHINGTON

The President of the United States takes pleasure in
presenting the NAVY CROSS to

LIEUTENANT NATHANIEL M. DIAL
UNITED STATES NAVY

for service as set forth in the following

CITATION:

"For heroism in combat with the enemy during the
period December 7, 1941 to March 18, 1942, as Commanding Officer of the U.S.S. NAPA. While exposed
to frequent horizontal and dive bombing attacks by
enemy Japanese air forces, Lieutenant Dial directed
the anti-aircraft batteries of his ship and conducted
operations of strategic importance involving hazardous
missions such as to bring great credit to his command
and the United States Naval Service."

For the President,

Frank Knox

Secretary of the Navy.

TOP: The official citation for Minter's Navy Cross

BOTTOM: USS *Napa* logbook entry for December 8, 1941, with the handwritten note "Received word that hostilities with the Japanese Empire
had started"

IMPERIAL JAPANESE ARMY

1. I am interned at the Philippine Military Prison Camp #1

2. My health is — excellent; good; fair; poor.

3. I am — injured; sick in hospital; under treatment; not under treatment.

4. I am — improving; not improving; better; well.

5. Please see that your health

is taken care of.

6. (Re: Family) All my love (210 lbs) to you and children.

7. Please give my best regards to John B. Body, 356-7 Page St., Garden City, N. Y.

REPORT OF CASUALTY
NAVPERS-2059 (REV. 1-45)

10788

NAME (Last)	(First)	(Middle)	RANK OR RATING	BRANCH	STATUS	FILE OR SERV. NO.
DIAL	Nathaniel	Minter	Lt.	USN	Active	

CASUALTY CONTROL NO.	DUTY ATTACHMENT		CASUALTY STATUS			
34894-Y-83-7	Staff Commandant 16th Nav.Dist.		Prisoner of War to Dead			

CASUALTY CODE	ENEMY ACTION	CAUSE OF CASUALTY		
6800 to 8321	Yes	Enemy Action		

DATE OF CASUALTY	PLACE OF CASUALTY		AREA
14 Dec. 1944	Manila Bay Area--At Sea		Asiatic

DATE OF APPT. OR ENLIST.	PLACE OF ENLISTMENT		PREVIOUS DUTY
18 July 1928			USS NAPA

STATE CREDIT	(Street)	(City)	(County)	(State)	NAVAL DISTRICT
1852 Kalorama Rd. N.W.	Washington		D. C.		

DATE OF BIRTH	PLACE OF BIRTH	(City)	(State)	MARITAL STATUS	DEPEND.	RACE
21 Mar. 1911	Laurens		S. C.	Married		White

NOTIFICATION OF NEXT OF KIN

By Local Activity	By Letter	By BuPers / By Telegram 5-0	No Notification

NAME(S) OF NEXT OF KIN	RELATIONSHIP(S)	ADDRESS(ES)
Elizabeth P. Dial	Wife	325 Claremont Ave., Long Beach, Calif.
Nathaniel Victor Dial	Son	Same
Diana Dial	Daughter	Same
Mrs. N. B. Dial	Mother	1852 Kalorama Rd., Washington, D.C.
Mrs. Grace Porter	Mother-in-law	1256 East Ocean Bend, Long Beach, Calif.
Mrs. Matthew Perry	Sister	2607 31st St. N.W., Washington, D.C.

Evidence establishing death under
Public law 408 rec'd 28 July 1945

DATE	SUPERSEDING REPORT
7 Aug. 1945	22 Oct. 1945 (SS)

TOP: Minter's Red Cross Card with the cryptic message for "John B. Body"

BOTTOM: Official Report of Casualty for Minter, received on November 14, 1945 (and incorrectly listing the date of death as December 14, 1944)

Dec. 12, 1944
Old Bilibid Prison
Japanese Prison Camp
#5 - Manila P.I.

Sweetheart darling,

This is being written on the eve of leaving the above camp for another one probably in Japan proper. There is much to say but time is limited and I know that the things which are really important between us (and there are so many wonderful ties) are part of our very beings and need no telling. I have received six letters from you - including the one in which you acknowledged my "rooster" message. Needless to say that was a thrill. So far I have had only the two small snaps of Victor & Diana. Please send lots and lots of pictures including your dear self. I will leave this here with a friend in hopes that

Minter's last letter, December 12, 1944

TOP: Aerial shot of the *Enoura Maru* bombing, January 1945

BOTTOM: Warwick P. Scott, one of Minter's bunkmates at Cabanatuan Prison, and uncle of the author's mother

TOP: Cdr. William Ruffin Cox, 1945 (courtesy of Tudy Hill)

BOTTOM: Cdr. Doug Fisher (courtesy of John Littig Jr.)

Minter II's children at Olongapo Bay hell ship memorial, 2008

Hug the children close and tell them I adore them. You too must keep brave! And I will. We will be together again—and have a life brimming with happiness. Until then—chin up! You are my life! My love! My all!

Yours for always.

Minter

The poem *Love* by Roy Croft contains these lines:

> I love you,
> Not only for what you are,
> But for what I am
> When I am with you.
> I love you,
> Not only for what
> You have made of yourself,
> But for what
> You are making of me.
> I love you
> For the part of me
> That you bring out;
> I love you
> For putting your hand
> Into my heaped-up heart
> And passing over
> All the foolish, weak things
> That you can't help
> Dimly seeing there,
> And for drawing out
> Into the light
> All the beautiful belongings
> That no one else had looked
> Quite far enough to find.
> I love you because you

Are helping me to make
Of the lumber of my life
Not a tavern
But a temple;
Out of the works
Of my every day
Not a reproach
But a song.
I love you
Because you have done
More than any creed
Could have done
To make me good
And more than any fate
Could have done
To make me happy.
You have done it
Without a touch,
Without a word,
Without a sign.
You have done it
By being yourself.
Perhaps that is what
Being a friend means,
After all.

So, in someone else's lyrical words, as he had done so often by reading aloud with her, Minter told Lisa of his feelings for her— feelings that would survive whether he did or not.

MINTER GAVE THE letter over to his friend who was not summoned to board that day, Maj. H.F. Bertram of the US Army; shook his hand solemnly; and wished him Godspeed. Then Minter turned to join the line of prisoners shuffling out, blinking in the light to see what awaited them.

The prisoners (who, as well as US troops, were also comprised of several dozen Dutch, Czech, and English men) included many men who were or had recently become good friends to Minter. He was close with his former Annapolis classmate Shields Goodman, his prison barrack mate Ken Wheeler, Perroneau Wingo of the *Napa*, and John Elliot of the *Canopus*, but in particular had formed a tight triumvirate of friendship with John Littig and Doug Fisher. Littig and Fisher were part of Naval Intelligence until the fall of Manila, whereupon they had dumped US currency into Manila Bay, burned the paper money, and set off for Corregidor aboard President Quezon's yacht rather than risk capture by the Japanese.

These men were herded through the walled city and paraded out to Pier 7 where a 7,300-ton Japanese passenger ship was docked. On its side was the designation *Oryoku Maru*. Taylor, the chaplain, felt a jolt of hope that maybe the trip to Japan wouldn't be as bad as they all feared. The *Oryoku Maru*, built around 1930 as a passenger liner, was in good shape, and he was sure it had first- and second-class cabins that would be a huge step up from the conditions in which he and the other prisoners had been living.

Taylor's first perceptions quickly changed as he looked around the pier. A group of approximately two thousand Japanese civilians—men, women, and children—approached the ship. This well-dressed group was comprised of the professionals—accountants, clerks, engineers, and diplomats—who had been running the country during the occupation and were now trying to get themselves and their families home while there was still time. As Taylor watched, the *Oryoku Maru*'s captain welcomed them up the gangplank, bowing slightly to each family. Taylor knew *they* were the people destined for the first- and second-class cabins. That meant only one place remained for the prisoners—the hold of the ship.

His and the other prisoners' hearts sank further as they looked around the harbor.

Manny Lawton, a prisoner from South Carolina, described the scene: "Bomb-blasted rusting hulks, some listing heavily, some upright with water washing over their decks, others identifiable only by smokeless stacks reaching helplessly toward the sky."[7]

With disturbed hearts, recalled Chaplain Taylor, "The men milled restlessly on the dock as though it were the night before an execution."[8]

They might have been better off if it had been.

After several hours of standing in the oppressive heat, around 3 p.m., the prisoners began loading in. Their Japanese captors were visibly nervous and in a hurry to get underway before American planes returned. They prodded the prisoners with rifle butts and sharp commands to descend the narrow staircase into the light-less holds below. Inside, the air was stagnant—stale and heavy from a lack of ventilation—and the addition of 1,619 unwashed men soon added to the stink.

The hold had a low ceiling that prevented the men from standing upright. Minter and fellow Annapolis classmate Shields Goodman were roughly shoved down the ladder, in turn pushing the men who had gone before. The temperature in the hold rose, exacerbated by the sun beating on the sides of the metal ship, making it too hot to touch. It burned the skin of the prisoners trapped up against it by the bodies of the others. It was pitch dark with only one beam of sunlight from the hatch's aperture.

"The heat was indescribable, unbearable," said Taylor. "We perspired profusely and became gripped by a gnawing thirst."[9]

The only air came from a shaft, perhaps twelve square feet, in the center, and the lack of oxygen soon became a physical danger. Men began passing out, unable to fall, collapsing on the man standing next to them in the dark. Men started to pant like animals, and the sound added to the rising wave of panic filling the holds. Some prisoners began screaming, and the contagion spread. The Japanese interpreter, Shusuke Wada, peered down into the hold and warned the prisoners that they were disturb-ing the Japanese passengers. If they continued to make noise, he would close the hatch, he hissed.

The men got quieter; but when the ship weighed anchor and its great engines turned over and slipped away from the dock, a cry of panic again went up from the hold. True to his word, Wada slammed the hatch shut. That weak ray of light and any breath of air disappeared. It must have felt to Minter, entombed in the most crowded hold, that he was in his coffin. He closed his skeletal fist around his Annapolis ring and tried to control his own screaming.

Around him, the prisoners went wild, pushing and heaving toward the ladder leading upward. It was pandemonium. Fighting his way through, Cdr. Frank Bridget, a Navy man, swung himself to an upper rung on the ladder and shouted, "Gentlemen, we're in this thing together, and if any of us want to live, we're going to have to work as one. If we panic, we're only going to use up more precious breaths of oxygen—we're all going to calm down."

One of the prisoners would recall Bridget's calm leadership at that moment. "He saved us with his voice."[10]

Bridget instructed the men to take off any clothing they had and fan air toward the back of the hold where men were literally suffocating in the heat. Then he climbed the ladder, cracked the hatch, and told Wada he was coming up to talk to him. Wada allowed him to and listened when Bridget told him men were dying from lack of air and water. The prisoners who had passed out had to be brought to the deck to revive. The hatch needed to be opened, and buckets of water had to be lowered to those below, Bridget explained. Unexpectedly, Wada agreed with all of the requests, and men were hauled up, over the heads of their fellows, to lay four at a time on the deck, where they regained consciousness. A little water and some rice were passed to those below, and the *Oryoku Maru* steamed on.

The ship was nearing Mariveles when the sun went down. Total darkness engulfed the holds, and men lost their grip on sanity. They turned on each other like rabid dogs, beating and strangling each other, slipping in the excrement that fouled the hold, tearing open veins to drink the blood of the fellow prisoners. To slake their insatiable thirst, they drank their own urine. The horrible sounds of strangulation, screaming, and cries to their mothers and their god resounded off the sides of the metal hull, adding to the din of the damned.

When morning brought weak rays of light back to the hold, those left alive surveyed a scene of horror. Fifty men had died of thirst or heat or violence, and many of those alive were at the brink of death, with red-rimmed eyes, unable to weep for lack of tears. Some stood as still as corpses themselves. Those who could move helped stack the dead in a pile beneath the hatch.

Their ghastly labor was interrupted at around 9:00 a.m. when the ship's anti-aircraft gunners started firing. American bombers off the USS *Hornet* had found the *Oryoku Maru* and were coming in fast, guns blazing, on strafing runs. Their .50-caliber bullets angled down the hold, ricocheting off the walls and wounding several prisoners. Bombs exploded in the water all around the ship. Frank Bridget took his place at the top of the ladder and narrated the action to those below as calmly as if he were announcing a Yankees game on the radio.[11] "Here comes another one, boys... he's getting closer... duck!"

The prisoners cheered for the planes.

"Give 'em hell! Pour it on!" they yelled, heedless of their own safety now, exhilarated that the US planes were raining hot lead down on the Japs's heads.

There were nine booming successful bombing runs. One rent a jagged hole just above the waterline in the side of the *Oryoku Maru*, and a concussion was felt in the stern of the ship. The rudder had been damaged, and the ship ran aground at Olongapo Point in Subic Bay.

All through that night, the prisoners could hear their captors off-loading the Japanese passengers to lifeboats and ferrying them to shore. American doctors were summoned from the hold to treat wounded passengers, but no water or food was sent to the men dying in the darkness.

The screaming began again, and some men fell on the pile of stacked corpses to drink their blood. In the pandemonium that followed, several of the prisoners committed suicide, tearing at their own flesh until they bled to death.

In the morning, December 15, Wada yelled down to the remaining prisoners to get ready to swim to shore, three hundred yards away. As they were organizing into groups, they heard the sound of Navy dive-bombers overhead. The plane's second pass dropped a string of bombs, and one scored a direct hit to the aft hold, where Minter was held. The *Oryoku Maru's* stern was blasted off, and a fire started in the hold. About one hundred men died instantly.

The remaining men streamed toward the ladder, pushing and shoving to pull themselves up. Japanese guards at the top fired into the pile of men, and the dead fell back down into the hold. Prisoners scrambled over their bodies. Those who made it to the deck began waving their arms and signaling wildly to the fighter planes overhead to draw attention to the fact that they, too, were Americans. Unfortunately, several planes strafed the hapless swimmers, thinking they were Japanese troops. Finally, the pilot in the lead plane seemed to understand and waggled his aircraft's wings in acknowledgment before peeling off. His squadron followed and banked off over Subic Bay.

The prisoners threw themselves over the side into the warm waters of the bay. Those who had been injured in the bombing runs gasped as the salt water hit their open wounds. Though weak and shaken, Minter made it under his own power those three hundred yards. Those who couldn't swim were herded by the guards' weapons poking their backs. Those already in the water swam to help their comrades. Minter's friend, Ken Wheeler, returned three times to the ship to help others swim ashore. Any who deviated from a narrow lane defined by the guards' machine-gun fire were shot in the water. Two seamen made use of the chaos to swim away, finally coming on shore several miles down the coast, where they made good their escape. They were the lucky ones.

All told, of the original 1,619 prisoners, 1,340 made it to shore.[12]

Guards prodded the prisoners to an area adjacent to a single tennis court where, ironically, Minter had played during his early days in Manila. He would now spend some of the worst days and nights of his life there.

Nearby was a water tap with a trickle coming out of the spigot. Men were allowed to fill their canteens but had to stand in line for nearly six hours to do so. For roughly half of the prisoners, this was the first water they'd had in three days. Many got none at all, as Wada arrived and had the men marched on to the tennis court so they could be checked against rosters.

Encased by chicken wire, the tennis court didn't have enough space for the men to lie down, so the men lined themselves up on the faded court lines, facing each other such that, sitting on the ground, one's legs were outstretched between the open legs of the man opposite. Under the baking sun, they watched as Navy planes returned and sank the *Oryoku Maru*. When the hell ship keeled over, the men still capable of speech gave a ragged cheer.

No food was issued on December 15 or 16, and the water situation did not improve. On the evening of the seventeenth, one woefully inadequate sack of uncooked rice was issued, enough only for 130 prisoners. Spread among the 1,340, this amounted to about two tablespoonsful for each man. The same amount of rice was issued on the eighteenth and nineteenth. On the twentieth, the ration increased to four tablespoonsful. All of this was eaten raw, although facilities for cooking were stored close by and within sight.

The starved, thirsty, and wounded men were mostly naked and, with no provision to protect them from the heat and blazing sun of the day or the cold temperature at night, men were suffering from exposure. Those who had shirts shared their pants with the naked. Those suffering from severe sunburn were given hats by their fellow prisoners to offer some relief.

A small area had been set aside for the wounded, but no supplies were available. One marine, whose shrapnel wound turned gangrenous, had his arm amputated with a razor blade, as a doctor nicked away his flesh and bone while other prisoners pinned him down screaming. He survived only a few days. About a dozen men died during the six days the prisoners were detained on the tennis court and were buried just outside it.

The remaining doctors, faced with no supplies or medicine, begged their captors to allow the most seriously wounded to return to Cabanatuan or Manila for treatment. Wada finally agreed, and fifteen American casualties, including Minter's friend, John Elliot, were put on a truck and driven off over the Zambales Mountains. They weren't returned to either Cabanatuan or Manila, however. At a remote spot in the jungle, they were thrown off the truck, lined up, and systematically bayoneted and decapitated. Their remains were buried in a shallow grave discovered after the war.[13]

On the morning of December 20, five hundred of the men were taken by train to San Fernando, Pampanga. The second group left on the twenty-first. Along the way, Minter's close friend, Jack Littig, part of a gang of three along with Doug Fisher, died. The first group was placed in the provincial jail and the second group in the movie house. While there, the prisoners were finally issued a tiny portion of rice.[14] There was a spigot with running water at both the theater and the jail, and the men were at last able to slake their raging thirst.

On Christmas Eve, the prisoners were moved again, this time to the railroad station where they were loaded into boxcars, 180 men to a car—a near physical impossibility. To make the numbers work and to act as human shields against any US bombing runs, forty of the sickest men were placed on top of the cars. Inside, due to the heat and crowding, men began passing out from lack of air. With no space to fall down, they collapsed against their fellow passengers who tried to lift the men overhead, hand-to-hand, to revive them closer to the boxcar's entrance.

The train arrived at San Fernando, La Union, on Christmas morning, in weather that was bitterly cold. The ragged, barefoot, and nearly naked prisoners were marched to a schoolhouse a half a mile away and ordered to dig for water. After digging five feet below the surface, they found water, and doctors poured the last of their iodine into the holes in an attempt purify it. The men knelt, cupped their hands, and drank the muddy water.

Orders were soon received that the men were to line up and prepare for a march to the beach. The prisoners stayed on the beach, alternately baking and freezing for two days and nights, after which a first group of 236 men was loaded aboard the *Brazil Maru*, an old 2,500-ton freighter. The remainder of the men, including Minter, boarded the *Enoura Maru*, a ten-thousand-ton freighter, formerly used to transport cavalry horses. The floor of the hold was lined with fouled straw, and flies covered the piles of manure scattered everywhere. Lice-ridden and stinking, the hold was also freezing and damp. During the six-day trip to Takao, Formosa, the men received one mess kit of rice and one half cup of soup to be split between four men. Both were lowered in a bucket and soon covered in black flies. After a few days, the Japanese stopped feeding them all together. "American submarines sink our supply ships—no food for you!" their captors yelled to the starving men. Four to five of the men died every day.[15] Minter's friend and second in command of the *Napa*, Ens. Perroneau Wingo, would be one of them.

Some of the others were hanging onto life by the thinnest of threads. Many were too weak to eat, and their buddies held their heads up and lowered the cup to their lips. A Catholic priest, Fr. Bill Cummings,[16] went from man to man, baptizing them with his own spit.[17] Sixteen more died and were thrown overboard, their bodies weighted with stones.

On New Year's Eve, December 31, 1944, the *Enoura Maru* dropped anchor in the port of Takao. The wounded Japanese who had been transported above decks were loaded onto barges and taken ashore. The American prisoners were left in the hold for nine more nightmarish days. While the Japanese celebrated the New Year, the prisoners were left in the hold to fend for themselves. Disease was rife. Men kept dying of starvation and desperation. On January 6, the remaining 230 men on the *Brazil Maru* were transferred over to the *Enoura Maru*, further cramping space and taxing the scarce food and water resources.[18]

On January 9, the same morning that American forces were landing at Lingayen Gulf in the Philippines, the drone of planes and anti-aircraft fire was heard by the men on the *Enoura Maru*. Almost simultaneously, the whistle of bombs pierced the air. The *Enoura Maru*, tied up in a two-ship nest, was a plum target for the American bombers. The ship was rocked violently from a near miss, causing a flail of bomb fragments and steel fragments from the sides of the ship. The bomb killed about three hundred outright and injured many more. Minter was among the wounded. A razor-sharp piece of shrapnel pierced his lung through his left ribs, and a huge gash in his shoulder began gushing blood in a torrent. Frank Maxwell, a pharmacist's mate from the *Napa*, along with Minter's good friend Doug Fisher, were dazed but unhurt in the bombing and rushed to the old skipper's side. Maxwell knew what he was seeing. An artery had been severed, and each beat of Minter's heart pumped out more of his lifeblood. Maxwell frantically ripped off the dirty rags he was wearing and stuffed them into Minter's wound. Assisting Maxwell, Fisher tried pulling the jagged shrapnel out of Minter's side, but that only caused more bleeding. Maxwell kept applying pressure to the shoulder wound. Fisher felt helpless. He sat back as the noise from the bombers grew more distant. In the lull, Minter grabbed Fisher's hand and with surprising strength pulled himself almost upright.

"Doug, this is it for me. I'm not going to make it home," Minter said. Pulling his Annapolis ring off a shred of material dangling between his skeletal legs, Minter pressed it into Fisher's hand.

"Make sure this gets to Lisa for me, will you? Promise me you'll get the ring home. Tell her I loved her, will you, Doug?"

Fisher looked at his eyes and saw that Minter was right. He was not going to make it home. Doug promised that he would get the ring safely back to Lisa and then watched as Minter took his last breath. He closed his friend's eyes.[19]

The scene was Dantesque within the hold of the crippled *Enoura Maru*. One of the bombs had scored a direct hit on its target. Splintered decking crashed down on the men in the hold, followed by a huge steel girder. The massive weight pinned a hundred prisoners to the floor of the hold. Manny Lawton recalled the scene when the dust settled: "... Tangled, grotesque positions of violent death ... limbs ripped from bodies and hands and torsos wrested apart."[20] The surviving men had tried to help those trapped, but the girder couldn't be moved. They would stay in the hold three more days listening to the lessening screams of agony from those trapped beneath the steel. On the fourth day, the Japanese arrived with a crane to lift the girder then gather the bodies, including Minter's, in giant nets like so many dead fish. They were then buried in a mass grave at a beach four miles away.

The bombing of the *Enoura Maru* claimed more than four hundred American lives. Some 161 men died upon arriving in Japan, in the middle of winter, where the mistreatment, malnutrition, and slave labor continued until liberation. Of the 1,619 men who were prisoners on the *Oryoku Maru*, *Brazil Maru*, and *Enoura Maru*, just 372 survived the war. Even then, the life expectancy of the survivors was dramatically lower than for other surviving veterans.

In preparation for the war crimes trial, Alva C. Carpenter, Chief of the Legal Section, GQ, Supreme Commander of the Allied Powers, made the following statement:

"Of all the cases of brutality and mistreatment accorded prisoners of war that have come out of World War II, none can compare with the torment and torture suffered by our soldiers (and sailors) who were prisoners of war aboard the ships, *Oryoku Maru, Brazil Maru,* and *Enoura Maru* . . . on that voyage from Manila to Japan. . . . It is a saga of men driven to madness by sadistic captors." [21]

Survivors of this hellacious journey had difficulty in talking about their experience. As recounted by one survivor, "When you speak of the good and the heroic, don't talk about us. The generous men—the brave men—the unselfish men—are the men we left behind." [22]

— 9 —

IN RESEARCHING MY grandfather's life, I have so far under-
taken four separate trips to the Philippines in order to try to
piece together the facts of his story, to imagine the hell he
suffered, and to know I had walked where he had walked and seen
with my own eyes some time-distorted version of the last vistas
he ever saw.

My first visit to the Philippines was in 2000. At that time, I
hadn't really discussed the project with my father, and I made
the journey alone as a four-day layover after a business trip to
Japan and Hong Kong. The arrival into Manila the first time felt
decidedly uncanny. Even on the approach to the Manila airport,
it quickly became clear how busy—and poor—Manila was. Being
physically present where he had stood, I distinctly felt that I was
getting closer to Minter. I had a checklist of locations to visit, keen
to follow in his footsteps and conjure his presence, including Bilibid Prison where he had twice been locked away, now a holding
station for some sixteen thousand people awaiting trial, and Pier 7,
where he had come into Manila for the first time on SS *Garfield* in
1941, and also where he boarded the *Oryoku Maru* three years later.

At Corregidor, the sensation of being closer to my grandfather
became stronger, especially when I visited the Malinta Tunnel,

where he spent his last few hours as a free man, before the capitulation in May 1942. The Malinta visit included an animated sound and light show, a simulation of what it may have looked and sounded like for those who were cooped up during the bombardments. I walked around with reverence, making idle talk with other American tourists and devouring the history and anecdotes. Never had a WWII site been more meaningful to me.

A year later, the events of September 11, 2001, would nudge me to reveal all to my father, and within a short time of reading the manuscript, he asked me to arrange a second trip. This time, we were determined to honor his father together.

For the second trip, in December 2004, we were a party of four: my father, Victor; my half-brother, William; my sister's husband, Dr. Shamus Carr, MD, USN; and me. This time we began by paying our respects at the American War Cemetery, the largest such facility outside of the United States, with seventeen thousand service men and women laid to rest there and a huge wall providing the names of an additional thirteen thousand missing. We found the name of Ens. Perroneau Wingo, Minter's executive officer on the *Napa*; and that of Lt. Warwick Scott, the brother of Minter II's great uncle Edgar Scott, also captured at Corregidor, and who was killed on the *Oryoku Maru* hell ship.

Again, we visited the Bilibid prison—this time getting to see its vastly overcrowded horror up close after being granted an inside tour—and the tunnels of Corregidor. On this trip, we also went to the former Army Navy Club, with its pre-war clubhouse and two tennis courts. I saw my father visibly affected here and wondered if he felt Minter's presence, and was thinking of those long, loving letters to Lisa describing how he'd spent his time there between his arrival in the Philippines in September 1941 and the outbreak of war, playing tennis on those very same dusty courts.

Driving south down the Bataan Peninsula, we realized we were traveling part of the route taken by American and Filipino POWs following their surrender in April 1942 on the infamous Death

March. The month of December is a "cool" month and the start of the dry season; nevertheless, we were uncomfortably hot and complained about it. April is the hottest month of the year, and the driest. The road taken by the POWs included several climbs, and, considering their weakened condition after months of fighting, the lack of water and food, and the ubiquity of malaria, dysentery, or both, it was easy to see how awful things must have been. What had been until then a somewhat abstract historical event became a vivid, real-life horror.

But the main focus of this trip was for us to find a way to pay our respects. We hired a boat to motor to the place where the *Oryoku Maru* lies, ten fathoms deep and about three hundred yards offshore. Here, on December 15, sixty years to the day after the sinking of the ship, we laid wreaths and sang the naval hymn "Eternal Father." My father concocted a plan to commission a memorial plaque for Minter.

In 2008, I returned yet again to the Philippines, this time just my father and me. The main purpose of our trip was to inaugurate the memorial plaque and to visit the elegant Hell Ship Memorial at Olongapo—the brainchild of Duane Heisinger,[1] another man who lost his father—for those who faced peril in those miserable and deadly voyages.

Returning for a fourth trip with my wife and two children the week after Christmas 2008, I soaked up the local atmosphere when the kids and I went to the gorgeous and rolling hills of Banaue and walked down the ravine to visit with some local tribes-people. We were given a royal welcome and feasted on homemade foods, observed the slaughter of a pig, and were dressed in local garb. As is so often the case, the poorest people are the most generous. It was a marvelous experience; the older grandmother took us in and made us feel like her own.

Thence, we went to Olongapo in Subic Bay to visit the site where the *Oryoku Maru* was sunk. Having been thrice before, it was fun to retrace my own footsteps, as well as to recount to my family how and where my grandfather had been. As I photographed my children in front of the memorial plaque, the very existence of which was a result of so many years of research and a burning need to make some sign of thanks and remembrance, I felt a sense of fulfillment and satisfaction. This was to be unfortunately short-lived.

A few years later, after continuing to work on this book and on a documentary about my grandfather, recently declassified documents[2] proved to me that my grandfather did not actually die after the sinking of the *Oryoku Maru* on December 15, 1944, but as I have told it here (and as Doug Fisher confirmed) after the bombing of the *Enoura Maru* on January 9, 1945. This fact took many years to come to light. We had so many contradictory versions of this story, each backed up with evidence and even first-hand accounts. Documents—both official and unofficial—as well as memories and memoirs contradicted one another. Not only had our moving memorial a few years earlier taken place on the wrong date; but we were not even in the right place, since I was now able to determine that the location of Minter's death was actually in Taiwan. Intriguingly, the declassified documents showed that his body had been one of just twenty-seven out of 429 bodies to be positively identified in a 1949 exhumation of the mass burial site.

As a result, I was forced to revisit my narrative. This discovery created a fair amount of hand-wringing. For starters, the memorial plaque my father had commissioned now displayed an inaccurate date, and I would have to reshoot to correct this information in the documentary film. More poignantly, we had to accept that our family journey in 2004 was no longer the perfectly appropriate moment it once seemed.

More than anything else, this mad tangle of information brought home to me how hard it is to separate fact from fiction when dealing with wartime events, even with seventy years to get the record straight. In 1945, Lisa and her children had nothing but the occasional update from the Red Cross, the goodwill of Minter's colleagues, and a desperate, overwhelming need to believe that her husband would be coming home soon.

COMMUNICATIONS MAY HAVE been sparse; but in 1945, optimism was on the rise. After the capitulation of the Germans in May, the war in the Pacific was surely coming to a close. When Minter came home, Lisa knew, they would make it right. She would nurse him if he needed care. She'd make his favorite foods and keep the children quiet so he could rest. When he was stronger, they could take Victor and little Diana to the playground and on long walks together. A picnic. She would pack a picnic. She would smother Minter with kisses and never again let him out of her sight. When Minter came home, all would be well.

Lisa lived on the edge, teetering between hysteria and hope. Friends and comrades stayed in touch with her, offering rose-colored glimpses of Minter's continued existence. For the past few years, it had been true that no news was good news. As long as she was sure Minter was alive, Lisa felt as though she could continue breathing.

Fannie Dodson cabled Lisa on April 8, 1945:

> Just visited Doctor Zandell at Naval Hospital. Here from Bilibid. Knew Minter well. He saw authentic list of casualties on December 1 ship. MINTER DEFINITELY NOT CASUALTY. Survivors sailed December from San Fernando for Formosa or Japan. Said Minter weights 175, brown, husky, and well. Letter follows.
> Fannie

Minter's own last letter, the one penned on his last night in prison before boarding the *Oryoku Maru*, had been left with Army Maj. Harold Bertram in the hopes he would see it delivered to Lisa. Bertram lived through the war and was liberated by American forces in April 1945. He would fulfill his promise and delivered both Minter's letter and one of his own to Lisa on July 7, 1945:

Major H. F. Bertram, MDC
Memphis Missouri
July 6, 1945
Dear Mrs. Dial:

Enclosed you will find a letter which your husband gave to me to be delivered to you before he was put on a Japanese ship and sent to Japan on Dec 13, 1944. Please accept my abject apologies for the long delay in delivering this but when he gave it to me I placed it in a bunch of rather important records—medical and otherwise—which were entrusted to me during the latter months of our imprisonment.

After our release I turned those records over to the Army Intelligence Dept. and I only yesterday was able to recover your letter and others, which I was to deliver. My negligence in not extracting those letters before I turned over the records is inexcusable and I apologize for it but we were under fire at the time and things are rather confused in an active combat area and my one thought at the time was to get the records, which really were important, back to a place of safety, where they wouldn't be destroyed by shells or fire nor lost.

I haven't read your letter so don't know how many of the many questions you have it will answer but I will assure you that Minter was in good health when I saw him last December. He had had amoebic dysentery about a year before but before he left for Japan I gave him a good supply of medicine for it just in case.

I am leaving for Calif. July 17th and will be there the evening of the 17th or 18th. Can be reached at 1062 E Howard St., Pasadena, c/o Capt. Homer T. Hutchinson—on the 20th I report to the Army Redistribution Center at Santa Barbara. If you would care to write me at either place [please do so] or if you prefer I would be glad to answer any of your questions if you could get to either place.

Sincerely yours,
Major Harold Bertram
Medical Corps, USA

Bertram's message was delivered with an accompanying letter from another prison camp contact, Lt. Cdr. George G. Harrison, USNR, a good friend of Minter's from even before the war:

5 April, 1945
Dear Lady,
    I am enclosing a card for you and his Mother, from your husband, who asked me to write to you as soon as I could upon my arrival in the States.
    He sends love and greetings, his only worry and concern is about your happiness, health and comfort. This message was written on the date of his transfer to Japan on 13 December, 1944. At that time he was in excellent health and good spirits, disappointed of course at being transferred, as it meant a longer time before he could be with you again.
    I trust that you have heard from him since then and that he will soon be home with his loved ones.
    Yours very sincerely,
    George G. Harrison

Safe. He was safe.

JULY 8, 1945
    It seemed to Lisa that the doorbell screamed instead of chimed. Or perhaps it was her own screaming she heard.
    When she opened the door and was handed the telegram, time and her breath stopped for a long moment. Then the pain hit, cold and hard as a fist in her stomach, and caused her to step back quickly. She dropped the telegram and would have fallen herself but for the messenger grabbing her elbows. He had delivered lots of these telegrams. Delivering such news never got easier.
    Minter was dead. Minter wasn't coming home again. Her children had no father. She was alone. Minter was dead, dead, dead—like a drumbeat in a nightmare, the phrase kept banging in her brain, "We regret to inform you ... "

Lisa collapsed and her mother, Grace, had to come fetch the children in the days that followed the news. Grace would be the one to tell the children their Daddy was in heaven. Lisa took to her bed, rising rarely.

She walked as though in a dream, wandering room to room, picking up framed photos, rearranging them endlessly, speaking out loud to pictures of Minter, before dissolving again in tears. Time passed strangely. Some days she slept until 3:00 p.m.; many nights she slept not at all.

A MESSAGE DELIVERED in person early in 1946 would break what was left of Lisa's heart. It was delivered by Cdr. Douglas Fisher, who had held Minter as he died in the hold of the *Enoura Maru*. Fisher had been one of the 372 survivors of that hellish forty-seven-day journey.

It was Fisher whom Minter entrusted with his Annapolis ring, begging him to see the ring safely into Lisa's hands.

Fisher remained in captivity—along with 150 other American prisoners—until October 3, 1945, bringing his number of days in captivity to 1,246, among the longest recorded for American soldiers up until that time.

After the war, Fisher recalled to his stepson,[3]

> "... I had gone through a great deal in trying to keep the ring through all that time, clear to Japan; but with our stringy clothing and so forth, it was quite a problem. I would tie it to one shred, and I would try to keep it here and there, and—having accomplished that thus far—I awoke one morning while I was in the hospital there [in Inchon] to find that it was missing.
>
> I suspected someone had taken it, because I had had it hidden in the slat below me. I couldn't find it at all, and I was much saddened by that and by not being able to return it to his wife. I went to see her sometime later in Long Beach, after my recovery, and told her about the situation, and she realized and was very nice about it."

As he departed the Dial home, Fisher handed his own wristwatch to Minter's son, Victor, who was nearly eight years old. He felt it was the least he could do. He had never seen such devastation in someone's eyes as he did in Lisa's.

WHEN MINTER'S DEATH had first been confirmed, Lisa fell apart. She couldn't stop crying, hold food down, nor sleep without an aid. Her nights were haunted by Minter as she replayed every moment they spent together, everything they had said, all the plans they had made. Consumed by incredible sadness, Lisa was barely recognizable as the lively, funny woman whose dazzling smile told her children how well-loved they were.

The people surrounding Lisa all tried to offer comfort—none more than Minter's mother, Jou-Jou:

WESTERN UNION
August 2, 1945
How my heart aches for you, Darling, only God knows, but while He created you of light and joy, he also endowed you with dauntless courage. This thought helps in the hour of supreme suffering. God comfort, bless and keep you and our precious babies, now and always...
Jou-Jou

. . .

September 23, 1945
Sunday afternoon
My darling child,
Words are not necessary between us, and I know how inarticulate one becomes when grief is too deep for tears! I wish I could put my arms around you and let us weep our hearts out together!

But you are young and lovely, and must guard your health: Minter would want you to save those sweet eyes he loved so dearly.

You and I together must fight that dreadful feeling of losing interest in life. Try to do something every day to divert your mind from this great blow. You are blessed to have those precious little ones whose wants require so much of your time and strength.

What a noble heritage our Darling left them and I know even up there, he is so proud of the faithful devotion you've given them in these lonely years!

Precious Grace has been a Rock of Gibraltar through the years helping you ride the baby life so pressing and plastic.

I feel I could hold them in my arms, hours at a time, and give them the sure knowledge of my love.

Children need so much love! I don't believe a child can have too much. It is their anchor.

Somehow, these days as they lengthen into weeks past, I can only keep track of time. I pray God will ease that stabbing pain in your heart and I hope soon we both can feel it is over, with the promise, "Thou wilt keep him in perfect peace whose mind is staid on Thee."

At Church this morning Mr. Myers sang, "O rest in the Lord; wait patiently for Him and He will give thee thine heart's desire." I've loved it and said it over thousands of times these long four years. It seems to bring a quietness to my soul.

Minter knows you will bravely carry on and each day his love and strength will surround you. You remember those beautiful lines?

"Thou art a Part protected
From Storms that round us rise
A garden interested
With streams of Paradise."

You are so dear and mindful to want me to keep the portrait (of Minter) awhile. I sit on the little love seat every day and feel his presence near, giving me courage. I will send it at any time you are ready.

Ruffin spoke of liking it more each time. He says it "grows on him." He came by to say goodbye as he left for Norfolk, but will be up several times before his destroyer goes out in November.

... Victor is such a bright, eager, dynamic child and as your mother says, so interesting. I know baby Diana is the joy of your life.... She's such a gentle, thoughtful little thing.

... Sometime, when you feel like it, let me have a message just to say you love me. We both are going through the severest test of our whole lives and our spirits are as close as breathing. Just know I'm thinking of you hourly and also that I hope to win the battle against becoming bitter, that would sully our lives.

Give darling Grace my love, she is such a wonderful friend. Tell her I shall answer her beautiful letter soon. I too find it almost impossible to write. I understand, precious daughter, and I am not in the least hurt. God bless you, and help you every hour of your lovely life.

Affectionately,

Jou-Jou

A letter also came from Don Francisco, the family friend who had hosted Lisa's marriage to Minter:

August 15, 1945
Dear "Lizibus,"

I have been thinking of you constantly these last few days, especially yesterday, your birthday. And I was in no mood... to join in the celebration of the war's end.

But today Peace has come, and someday, if not now, it must come to you. It is the dawn of a new day, the end of a tragic part. A new world lies before us all and we must learn to make the most of it. We must look ahead to new horizons. No one would wish us to do otherwise.

I am sending you my love and my strength, for even brave soldiers like you sometimes need both.

Affectionately,

Don [Francisco]

But peace didn't come to Lisa. She distracted herself with a futile mission to get a Navy ship named after Minter and an attempt to get his rank posthumously raised to lieutenant commander, which also failed. She also tried to show interest in the activities of the children, but nothing seemed to scratch more than just the surface of her grief. She sometimes turned to alcohol for solace, crying herself to sleep most nights. She felt like a ghost herself.

Her mother was worried. Lisa was depressed, skeletally thin, and drinking frequently. Grace convinced Lisa to go spend some time in New York with Don Francisco and his wife. Once there, in an effort to rekindle Lisa's love of life, Don saw to it that Lisa wasn't alone and tried to distract her with a never-ending social whirl of plays and parties. The children remained in California. Little Victor stayed with Grace, while Diana lived with a family who had two grown daughters.

Then, in what many considered unseemly haste, on November 2, 1946, on a cloudy and windy day, Lisa married Kennett Webb Hinks, a friend of Don Francisco's.

A graceful man from Minnesota, Kenn became surrogate father to the children and caretaker to Lisa. Her grief had become insupportable on her own. Kenn had served as an OSS officer during the war and knew the conflict's horrors. Though he had emerged with his well-known kindness and gentle sense of humor intact, and though he tried with infinite patience, he seemed unable to help his wife. Lisa never recovered her spirit. And no matter how hard he tried, Kenn was no replacement for Minter.

Lisa's son, Victor, recalls how, despite her new husband's kindness, Lisa was unable to get over her grief. He writes:

> My mother hadn't come to terms with my father's death. She'd occasionally assuage her sorrow with alcohol in front of Kenn, and sometimes my sister and me. She'd reminisce about her years with Minter and the love they'd had for each other. During these incidents, Kenn remained amazingly calm, always agreeing with her that Minter had been a great husband, a great father, and a great war hero.

My sister and I were greatly upset by these maudlin moments. I even began to repress thoughts about my father for fear
of causing more such incidents. Even when I was alone with my
mother, I cringed when she brought up my father, as she often
did, because it would usually end in tears. Although I spurned
her conversational overtures, buried deep inside me there was
grief for a father I never knew.

I was saddened by my mother's occasional bouts of depres-
sion. Fortunately Lisa mellowed as she grew older, and she
found a sort of peace alongside her saintly husband. She managed to hold her sadness within herself, but I know she never
stopped loving Minter. If there is a Heaven, it consoles me to
think that they're together again.

AFTER HIS BODY was repatriated, Minter Dial was reburied with
full military honors at Arlington Cemetery on July 15, 1949, on
a day that was stormy and blustery. Lisa, swathed in black and
leaning heavily on the arm of Kenn Hinks, stood at the graveside;
but Kenn, concerned that she would be unable to maintain her
composure, made the decision that Minter's children should not
attend the reburial. The traditional folded flag was given to Minter's mother, not Lisa.

At the reburial, Adm. Kenneth Hoeffel said of Minter in requiem:

"... He did not know what fear was. Of all my officers (none)
of them compared with him in those invaluable traits of man-
hood, courage, and ability to get things done during times of
stress. The Navy has lost a gallant, able, and courageous officer
in Minter and a dearly beloved friend ever to be remembered
with admiration and affection."

Jou-Jou never quite forgave Lisa for remarrying and placed an
obituary in the newspapers listing Minter as being survived by
only his mother and his siblings. No mention was made of Lisa
or Minter's children.

– 10 –

OUTSIDE OF INCHON, KOREA, MAY 1962

IT WAS DIRTY work, excavating the grounds of the former prison at Inchon. The shovel was raising new blisters on the hands of Yi Soo-young. Soo-young was slaving away next to his friend, Park Jong-yul, a former guard at the prison, in order to make a little side money. Looking down at his sore and filthy hands, he was sorry he didn't have a cushier job, like the one Buck Shin had. Buck was the driver of American Rear Adm. George Washington Pressey, Commander Naval Forces Korea, and he never had to do any backbreaking labor to earn his keep. In fact, the admiral treated Buck like family. He'd even been a guest at the admiral's table a time or two, an honor accorded very few Korean nationals.

Soo-young didn't agree with Jong-yul's opinions about Americans. Jong-yul thought they were "invading pigs" and made no bones about saying it—though not quite within earshot of any of the military brass around the place. He was no respecter of people or their possessions. When he and Soo-young had been gambling last night, Jong-yul even put up as his ante a gold ring that he'd found while digging in the mud. He showed it to Soo-young. It was heavy gold, inset with a blue stone. Soo-young didn't read much English, but he saw the year "1932" engraved on the side of the ring. What a lucky bastard Jong-yul was, thought Soo-young. That ring was probably worth a lot of money. When Jong-yul won the pot, he was headed straight to a pawnshop to collect and he'd go home with pockets full of cash.

After the game, Soo-young ran into Buck coming out of the admiral's residence, and, just to commiserate, he told Buck about the ring Jong-yul had found. Buck asked him to describe the ring again, as well as the number found on the outside. It sounded an awful lot like a ring the admiral himself wore. Saying goodbye to Soo-yung, Buck turned back to the house and went to find the admiral.

When he relayed what the ring looked like, the admiral listened with interest; but when he heard the number "1932," Admiral Pressey sprang into action, demanding Buck get the car immediately. When he had done so, the admiral jumped in and ordered Buck to take him, systematically but quickly, to every pawnshop in Inchon. In May 1962, there were 350,000 inhabitants in Inchon, and there were a vast number of small shops, most without significant signposts.

They searched every pawnshop, and their efforts were finally rewarded in one back-alley hovel, but they were almost too late. With Buck doing all the initial questioning, they heard that an American ring was recently sold to this particular pawnshop and had just been placed in the fire for melting. Pressey barked at the shopkeeper to take the ring out of the fire. The bottom of the ring had already caved in.

Pressey recognized the ring immediately. It was an Annapolis ring, Class of 1932, the same year he himself had graduated from the Academy.

Pressey said of Jong-yul: "In spite of my fastest work and in disobedience of counsel given the finder [working on former

US grounds], he pawned the ring at once. Although we redeemed it immediately, it was not before the pawnshop owner had defaced the back of the ring in his attempts to melt it and assay the gold. We are lucky that he was stopped before serious damage was done."

Particularly lucky because the name of the owner could still be seen.

Inscribed in the gold in flowing script was the name "Nathaniel Minter Dial."

Pressey was stunned. Minter Dial had been one of his closest friends at the Academy, his linemate on the lacrosse team for three years. Pressey had been one of Minter's ushers. And Betty Lee, Pressey's wife, had been Lisa's matron of honor when she and Minter were married, though they had since lost touch.

To have found Minter's ring in Inchon was astonishing.

Except for clean cracks in the gold on each side of the still-intact stone, the ring was even in good condition for having lain over seventeen years in the ground. Without discussion, Pressey handed over the equivalent of eighteen US dollars (142 dollars adjusted for inflation) for the ring and left the store, clutching the heavy gold in his hand. He could see Minter's face clearly before him, fancied he could even hear him laugh.

Pressey, who had spent the bulk of the war commanding the destroyer USS *Hobby* in the Pacific, knew his friend Minter had been a POW. After the war, he had even visited the Cabanatuan prison camp site where a scrap of paper with Minter's writing had been discovered. It read: "Oh God, how hungry... how tired I am."

Pressey knew his friend Minter had not survived the war and realized how important it was to get the ring back into Lisa's hands. He remembered that Minter had had a son who would now have been of age to join the Navy himself. Perhaps he could find Lisa through him?

Pressey searched the Naval Register and came across the name of Lt. (junior grade) Nathaniel (Victor) Dial—Minter's son. Victor had just finished spending two years on active duty as an officer in the Navy ROTC. Pressey immediately wrote to him. First, there was a letter. Then came a package.

Victor recalls:

On a warm and sunny day in June 1962, I was summoned to the post office of Haddonfield, New Jersey, to claim the registered package addressed to me by Rear Adm. George W. Pressey, Commander of US Naval Forces in Korea. Pressey had been one of my father's closest friends. I drove back to my temporarily rented apartment and prepared to see and touch my father's long-lost Annapolis class ring for the first time since I was three, when I would play with it on his hand.

But at this critical moment, I hesitated, then stopped. In a surprising moment of lucidity, I realized that this honor belonged not to me but to my mother. She'd learned from her late husband's prison-camp comrade, Navy Cdr. Douglas Fisher, how Minter had literally starved himself, refusing to trade his ring for food or water, just so that he could give his ring to the wife he loved so desperately. When Pressey had contacted me a few weeks before to announce how he'd literally unearthed my father's ring, he asked me where to send it. I'd impulsively asked him to send it to me, as my mother was in the process of moving to Charlottesville where she and Kenn (my stepfather) had just finished building their dream house. Better to send it to me, less chance of it getting lost—again.

Now that the little box was sitting there before my eyes, I saw more than ever that this was her moment. She should do it, or maybe we should do it together. I would be in New York for the coming weekend, and I'd see her there—we were deep into the planning of my forthcoming marriage in the fall.

Several days later, I handed her the box in New York. As she took it, tears were already streaming down her cheeks. She asked to be alone with the box and her thoughts. Kenn was nearby, and he gently suggested that the two of us let her deal with this emotional moment in her own way. We both knew how sensitive she could be when it came to Minter and their love affair, cruelly cut short.

Kenn and I sat in a nearby room and painfully listened to her sobs. After what seemed an eternity, she recovered her composure and proudly showed us the ring, and then there were three of us in tears.

The ring's return seemed to have brought with it the resurrection of Lisa's bottomless sorrow. She grew maudlin about what she had lost with Minter. On top of that, Lisa was struggling with cancer. Victor and Diana didn't know how to comfort their frail mother or quite how to feel about their dead father. The price of Minter's heroism was too dear to bear.

One Tuesday afternoon in early May of 1963, Lisa Dial Hinks was sitting alone in the living room of the comfortable house in Ivy, Virginia, that she and Kenn had lovingly designed and built for their retirement. Tuesdays were sometimes difficult for her because Kenn had accepted an offer to teach an economics class at the nearby University of Virginia, and it was the one day in the week he was away all day. On this particular Tuesday, Lisa was weighing the devastating news she'd received a few days earlier: her cancer had returned, and treating it would very likely lead to the loss of her second breast. Losing the first one four years earlier had been traumatic for Lisa, who cared so much about her femininity. The doctors at Sloan-Kettering had warned her that the cancer could recur at any time within a five-year window, and so it had. She knew first-hand what the surgery entailed, and dreaded the discomfort and disfigurement that was to come.

As she contemplated what remained of her life, she suddenly felt very lonely. When she was in this sort of mood, as she seemed more and more often to be these days, the stiff martini she held in her hand usually made her feel better; but for some reason, it didn't today. Maybe it was another rush of menopausal hormones that threw her so off-kilter. Or maybe it was that Victor had just a few months earlier married a Main Line girl and moved to Europe to work, or that Diana would soon be flying around the world with Pan American. Lisa's life's work—raising her children—was nearly complete. Kenn had been a kind, generous, devoted, and understanding husband; but deep down inside, she felt incomplete. Sure, Lisa had never had the chance to follow her dreams of becoming an actress. But something more important was missing. She knew what it was, of course. While Kenn and her children had given her great satisfaction, she realized once again that what she really wanted—what she must have—was the one thing she couldn't have in this life—her dear Minter. She was depressed at what lay ahead. She was so sad, so alone.

Suddenly she felt overwhelmed by great waves of nostalgia and grief. Fighting her growing despair was exhausting her. She was so tired. She decided to lie down for a moment in her cozy bedroom. Maybe she'd take a little nap. Even though she felt safer in her intimate boudoir, she took two pills to help calm her frazzled nerves. As she was carefully replacing the little bottle on her bedside table, she felt her weariness overtake her. She had waited for so long. So long between letters during the war, waiting for news, then so long afterward waiting for her broken heart to heal. She had even waited so long for his ring to come back to her, and now it had, and still nothing was different. What was left to wait for? He was never coming back. Never coming home. But she could go to him. She could go home to Minter. They could be together, at last—this time, forever. She took another couple of pills. Forever was getting closer.

After Lisa's death at just fifty-three years of age, the ring, which Kenn had mounted in a glass frame surrounded on each side by Minter's Purple Heart and Navy Cross,[1] passed on to Minter's son, Victor.

All Victor would ever have of his father and the last possession his father had touched before dying, the ring would become his greatest treasure.

IN EARLY 1967, Victor, with his family (my mother, Alix, pregnant with my sister, Lisa, and me) in tow, had just moved on a new assignment from Brussels to Paris, and was living in a beautiful mansion in Mareil Marly, on the outskirts of Paris. It was one of the perks of Victor's job as an expatriate executive at Ford Motor Company. The glass case containing his father's ring and medals held a place of honor in the library.

After a dinner at home, Victor and Alix retired to bed. As they slept, burglars made their way into the house. Apparently spooked, the intruders escaped in a hurry, taking only a few items. The silverware that had been left in plain sight on the dinner table was still there. A valuable pair of Boss shotguns was untouched. But the case with Minter's ring was missing.

It has never been found.

— 11 —

AFTERWARD

WORLD WAR II came to an official end on August 14, 1945. Though there were very few records to begin with, the Japanese destroyed the ones they kept on the Philippine prison camps and the hell ships in the war's aftermath. Most of the unofficial records, including prisoners' diaries and journals, were lost.

The International Military Tribunal for the Far East in Tokyo, Japan, was convened in April 1946 and heard the case against twenty-eight Japanese military and government officials accused of committing war crimes and crimes against humanity during World War II. The tribunal uncovered some horrifying statistics: Of 130,201 documented US military captured and interned during World War II, a total of 14,972 were killed while prisoners. However, the treatment was substantially different depending on the captor. Under German captivity, of the 93,941 POWs taken, 1,121, or 1.1 percent, were killed. Meanwhile, under the Japanese, of the 36,260 POWs taken, 13,851, or 38.2 percent, were killed.

Of all the Allied POWs who died in captivity, the Japanese were responsible for killing 93 percent of them. The ratio is even higher for those Americans taken in the Philippines, where the bulk of the prisoners were taken. Of 25,580 prisoners, an astounding 10,650 or 41.6 percent died as captives. Roughly 80 percent of the seventeen thousand Philippine Scouts who were captured died during the first year of captivity. Moreover, the conditions to which the POWs were subjected by the Japanese meant that the longevity of the survivors after the war was distinctly lower. In fact, as of January 1, 2000, the ex-POWs of Nazi Germany numbered 44,773 (48 percent of the survivors) versus only 5,745 (16 percent of survivors) for the ex-POWs of the Japanese.[1] By all accounts, the treatment of the less well-equipped and less sturdy Filipinos was as uncivilized. At the surrender of Bataan, some sixty thousand Filipinos were captured. Of these, fully twenty-seven thousand died within the first two months of captivity. The Americans were in better shape, but survival was as much a question of age and luck as it was physical fitness. The men were easy prey to disease, much less the unprovoked, gratuitous acts of violence and murder committed by the Japanese.

During World War II, all populations included, it is estimated that fifty million people were killed, with the Soviet Union losing twenty million (thirteen million soldiers and seven million civilians).[2] The German losses are estimated at 3.6 million civilians and 3.2 million combatants. The Japanese believed that two million civilians and one million soldiers perished. The British and Commonwealth deaths are calculated at under five hundred thousand. The United States, with 291,557 battle deaths—and an astonishing 113,842 deaths from accident and disease—suffered the fewest casualties among the major nations. Just over 12 percent of these non-hostile deaths, however, came about in the prison camps.

On November 4, 1948, the war crimes tribunal ended with twenty-five of twenty-eight Japanese defendants being found guilty. Of the three other defendants, two had died during the lengthy trial, and one was declared insane. On November 12, the war crimes tribunal passed death sentences on seven of the men, including Gen. Hideki Tojo, who served as Japanese premier during the war, and other principals, such as Iwane Matsui, who organized the Rape of Nanking, and Heitaro Kimura, who brutalized Allied prisoners of war. Sixteen others were sentenced to life imprisonment, and two were sentenced to lesser terms in prison. On December 23, 1948, Tojo and the six others were executed in Tokyo.

In addition to the central Tokyo trial, various tribunals sitting outside Japan judged some five thousand Japanese guilty of war crimes, of whom more than nine hundred were executed. Some observers thought that Emperor Hirohito should have been tried for his tacit approval of Japanese policy during the war; but he was protected by US authorities who saw him as a symbol of Japanese unity and conservatism, both favorable traits in the postwar US view.[3]

Some thirty thousand Filipinos and 13,851 American POWs were killed by the Japanese. Each of those men left behind wives, children, mothers, and fathers—ripples in a pond of pain that would continue to affect their families and friends.

I REMEMBER ATTENDING my first American Defenders of Bataan and Corregidor (ADBC) convention in San Antonio, Texas.[4] The annual gathering had been going on since its inaugural session in January 1946. In the 1990s, these were attended by several dozen surviving veterans, men who had been there, had fought and surrendered, who had gone through the experience of over three years of imprisonment in vile conditions and were still willing and able to travel. These men were all over seventy years old. A few were in their eighties, men who were my grandfather's contemporaries. Alongside the veterans were direct and extended family members as well as a few friends and an occasional historian. The first time I went, I remember feeling very out of my league. I went alone. I had no family present. I had never been in the armed forces. I knew nothing of the decorum. Slowly, I was able to navigate through the event and started following up on leads to talk to the veterans who would most likely have been near or with my grandfather. One veteran, John Oleksa of the *Napa*, actually came looking for me, as he recognized the name. Shaking hands, speaking with these veterans who had possibly also shaken hands with my grandfather, was very grounding. Whenever appropriate, I grabbed my pen and paper and jotted down notes. However, at meal times, when the stories came fast and furiously, I was obliged to write down afterward what I could remember. It was almost overwhelming listening to people's stories in person, giving color to experiences I had only read about and imagined.

At the second ADBC convention, I was significantly better prepared and sought out the men I was looking for. I also had a chance to meet historians who were working on a major book. I felt like I had developed another circle of friends, united by a common passion to keep this part of history alive.

Outside of these conventions, once I had met some of the men and knew who to look for, I was also able to meet with some veterans and their families individually. In a race against time, I was fiendishly tracking down and following up on leads. Once I had found an address, the next trick was finding an appropriate way to connect and record any stories. This often involved writing letters. Otherwise, it was via telephone. In many of the cases, my main contact was a more able-bodied wife. I could feel how certain wives wanted to be protective of their husbands, careful to avoid conjuring up painful memories. When it was possible, I would make the trek to meet them in person. This was important for me for two reasons: Firstly, there is nothing more powerful than hearing the story live and in person. Secondly, I wanted to shake their hands and thank them in person, regardless of whether they had known my grandfather. I was so grateful for the way they welcomed me among them, sharing their stories and helping me to piece together my grandfather's life. And knowing what I now did of what these men had endured, I was even more grateful for their service and sacrifice.

CDR. DOUG FISHER, after visiting Lisa, went to visit the wife of John "Jack" Littig, the third of the triumvirate of friends. As with Minter, Doug Fisher promised to pass along Jack's dying wishes to his wife, Bettina. Doug ended up marrying Bettina (who was born in Manila to British parents and lived to be 101 years old) and became stepfather to John Littig Jr. Doug lived until 1972, when he died at the age of sixty-nine.

A 1932 graduate of Annapolis and originally from North Carolina, Adm. **Ruffin Cox** was my father's godfather and, in the follow-up research, we discovered that the Cox-Dial association went back further than one could imagine. Ruffin's grandfather was Brig. Gen. William Ruffin Cox (1832–1919), who fought in the American Civil War with great distinction (and later became Secretary of the US Senate in Washington).[5] It turns out that General Cox was twice promoted to replace Gen. Stephen Dodson Ramseur (1837–1864). Ramseur was my great-great-great-uncle. Ramseur rose to the rank of major general and died at the age of twenty-eight while fighting in the Battle of Cedar Creek in 1864. Generals Cox and Ramseur were close comrades, as would be Ruffin Cox and Minter Dial eighty years later. Adm. Ruffin Cox was awarded the Navy Cross for "extraordinary heroism and distinguished service" while captaining the destroyer USS *McGowan* during the Battle of Surigao Strait, off the Philippine Islands on October 24 through 25, 1944.[6] Ruffin would live to be ninety years old and die in his bed in upstate New York on November 2, 1991, a day after bearing witness to the life and death of his friend Minter to me for this book. His wife, Tish, left a message on my voicemail, thanking me for having let him unburden his soul and die peacefully.

After WWII, Adm. **George Washington Pressey** had various missions that included being a teacher at the Armed Forces Staff College in Norfolk, Virginia, as well as serving in the training branch of the Bureau of Naval Personnel at the Pentagon. In May 1950, he was given the prestigious command of the battleship USS *Missouri* and served in the Korean War. After the Korean conflict, he remained in the service, being promoted to rear admiral in 1960 while serving as Chief of Staff of the 7th Fleet in Yokosuka, Japan. He was made Commander of US Naval Forces Korea (August 1960) and, in 1965, was confirmed as Deputy Chief of Staff for Military Assistance, Logistics, and Administration on the staff of Adm. U.S. Grant Sharp of the Pacific Military Command. He died while still in service on April 21, 1966, at the age of fifty-five. His widow, Elizabeth "Betty Lee," married Samuel D. Berger, Deputy US Ambassador of South Vietnam, and thus found herself stationed in Asia again. Betty Lee died in 2002, but not before I had the chance to connect with her and collect a few important stories.

In August of 2011, my grandfather Minter's story was the subject of a widely read *Smithsonian* article entitled *Minter's Ring: The Story of One World War II POW.*[7]

Then, in 2012, I received a Facebook friend request from a woman, Margy Wooding, whose name I did not recognize. Margy, it turned out, was the youngest daughter of Admiral Pressey. Her son, Jack, found me online doing some research about his grandfather for his mother. Jack had also helped Margy get onto Facebook and find me. The further serendipity of the timing of Margy's message was that it reached me two days before I was to make a speech about my grandfather's story in front of four hundred students at Sevenoaks School in Kent, England. In that speech, I was—as always—going to be referencing her father and his key part in the tale. To my astonishment, Margy said that she lived in England, only twenty miles from Sevenoaks. I invited Margy to my presentation, and she added a moving tribute to her father and the impact of his finding the ring on her family. In 2013, tragically, her son Jack, who had brought us together, was killed in a climbing accident in Scotland.

Bernard "Brute" Franklin Roeder was awarded the Distinguished Service Medal and five Legion of Merit medals with Combat "V" device. He served in the Korean War as vice admiral and died September 3, 1971, at age sixty.

Vice Adm. **Ken Wheeler**, who was born in Arkansas and raised in California, joined the Navy ROTC as an ensign out of the University of California, Berkeley, in 1939. He was a lieutenant (junior grade) when he was taken prisoner on Corregidor and was imprisoned in Cabanatuan along with Minter. For repeated acts of tremendous bravery, Admiral Wheeler was awarded the Distinguished Service Medal, three Bronze Star medals, two Legion of Merit medals, the Purple Heart, and Distinguished Unit Citations. After surviving the *Oryoku-Enoura-Brazil Maru* hell ship journey, he was shipped to Jinsen along with Doug Fisher, where he was liberated in October 1945. Admiral Wheeler had a standout postwar career, retiring in 1974 after thirty-five years of service. He retired in Statesville, North Carolina, where he was a highly involved civic leader. He died in April 2002 at age eighty-three.

About other crewmembers of the USS *Napa*:

John Oleksa Jr. was a career Navy man, retiring in 1960. He lived in Ohio with his wife, Mary, until his death in 2005 at age eighty-seven.

Austin Murdock recovered from his bad burns and survived his three years in captivity. When I finally tracked him down in April 1999, it was two months after his death. His wife, Elizabeth, of Seattle, Washington, wrote back a charming note saying, "[Austin] had many stories of the *Napa* and the Philippines and as a POW and, yes, of "Dial"—always the skipper—Dial—with great affection.... I wish you much luck in your endeavors. You will find nothing but love and devotion and great respect for your grandfather."

Cdr. **William "Gunner" Wells** enlisted in the US Navy in 1932. For his actions in WWII, he received several medals, including the Bronze Star. After the surrender on Corregidor, Wells was a POW for forty months. He retired in 1957 from the military and later became the manager of Bryant Hardware in Kempsville for twenty-eight years. He also served as a volunteer fireman for seventeen years with the Kempsville Fire Department and Rescue Service, where he was a charter member. He was married for fifty-two years to Dorothy M. Wells and died at the age of eighty-five in 1999.

CREW OF USS *NAPA*

Of the fifty-two US Navy personnel cited as being on the USS *Napa* under Minter, nineteen would die during the war. The bulk of the deaths occurred while being transported in one of the infamous hell ships.

NAME	TITLE AND SERVICE NUMBER	STATUS
Dial Lt. N. Minter	Commanding Officer 071326	KIA *Enoura Maru*, Jan. 9, 1945
Wingo Ens. P.B.	Executive Officer 96200	KIA *Enoura Maru*, Jan. 1, 1945
Letson Lt. (J.G.) Charles F.	Engineering Officer 063727	KIA *Shinyo Maru*, Sept. 7, 1944
Masa Rudoph E.	1st Lt, Warrant Officer 13141	Liberated from Bilibid Prison, Feb. 5, 1945—Died 1982
Grayson Elton	Asst. Engineering Officer 109993	KIA *Arisan Maru*, Oct. 24, 1944
Wells William	Chief Gunner's Mate 177093	Died 1999
Williams George R.	Chief Quarter Master 2146732	Died October 2014 (CA)
Puckett Vernon Fate	Chief Machinist Mate 3804068	KIA *Enoura Maru*, Jan. 9, 1945 (Grave)
Allen Carl Lee	Machinist Mate 2/c 2743678	Died 1993
Baffo Victor	Chief Water Tender 1/c 2717875	KIA Dec. 9, 1942 (Korea)
Bagwell William Claremondt	Water Tender 1/c 3466598	Died 1997 (TN)
Barrett Donald Patrick	Cox 2834746	KIA Feb. 4, 1943 (Japan)
Brodsky Charles	Chief Boatswain's Mate 2010101	KIA—Executed while attempting to escape on the *Arisan Maru*, Oct. 24, 1944

Collins Nathan Mayo	Machinist Mate 2/c 2681803	KIA *Arisan Maru*, Oct. 24, 1944
Craig Willard Homer	B Mate 2/c 3809265	KIA *Arisan Maru*, Oct. 24, 1944
Craven Jerry Albert	RM 2/c 3683616	Survived
Darneal Dillard Daniel	Machinist's Mate 2/c 3467011	Survived
Dodd William Donald	Carpenter's Mate 1/c 3810274	KIA, May 2, 1942
Franzen Roy Oscar	S 1/c 3816170	Survived, CA
Freeman Clarence A.	CC Std 2954429	Survived, TN
Grewcox Charles E.	Fireman 1/c 2503669	KIA Dec. 20, 1942 (Japan)
Haddon James Richard	CB Mate 3852434	Died June 1993 (WA)
Hambley Lewis Clark	SM 1/c 3719404	Died Jan. 16, 2005
Howard Robert Leroy	R Mate 1/c 196904	Died September 1987 (NY)
Hoyny Walter G.	B Mate 2/c 3285522	Died May 2000 (CA)
Ingram Osburn F.	S 2/c 2957538	Died February 2001
Keene Thomas Bradley	Gunner's Mate 1/c 4012680	KIA Feb. 10, 1943 (Osaka, Japan)
Kilmer Emmett Lee	EM 2/c 3371089	Died Nov. 4, 2002 (MO)
Leonhardt Corwin D.	Gunner's Mate 3/c 3001986	Died November 2000 (MI)
Love Wilbur Everett	S 1/c 3558520	Died March 21, 1998 (FLA)
Maxwell, Frank Lellwyn	Pharmacist Mate 2/c 2721782	Died Aug. 2, 1981 (FLA)
Mullis Fred William	S Mate 1/c 2950987	Died Oct. 19, 1979 (LCDR)–NC
Murdock Austin M.	Water Tender 1/c 2071168	Died 1999
Norket Jay Wiley	Gunners' Mate 3/c 2626196	Died 1982
Oleksa John Jr	Ship's Cook 2/c 2834229	Died 2005
Osborne John D.	Signalman 1/c 3719921	Died 1999 (IN)
Osborne Raymond D.A.	Radioman 1/c 3932475	KIA *Arisan Maru*, Oct. 24, 1944
Pitts Joseph L.	Fireman 1/c 2659566	KIA, Feb. 28, 1942
Plugge Lowell Jonathan	Yeoman 3/c 3165631	KIA Nov. 15, 1944 (Osaka)
Raz Andrew Alex	Water Tender 1/c 2834216	Died July 7, 1976
Richardson Harold Laverne	Machinist Mate 3/c 3213189	Died May 1999 (CA)
Robinson William F.	Chief Machinist's Mate 2913018	KIA Tokyo, POW, April 6, 1944
Snow Jep A.	Chief Machinist's Mate 198169	KIA Philippines, POW, Aug. 29, 1942

Swisher Morris Denver	Machinist Mate 3/c 3561111	Died March 10, 2003 (CO)
Tardif Paul Bernard	SEA 1/c 3111862	Died July 2004 (MI)
Taylor Harry Orlo	Chief Electrician's Mate 3717033	Died Dec. 27, 1987 (CO)
Tobias James E.	CB Mate 3808290	KIA Bilibid Prison, PI, Nov. 2, 1944
Washburn Roy McDonald	Water Tender 2/c 3759417	Died Jan. 8, 1973 (CA)
Watson D.H.	Chief Yeoman 2950999	Survived, Fukuoka POW Camp 1 Kashii Pine Tree Camp
West Lawrence Elmer	Radioman 3/c 3759363	Died 1978
West Max Lancaster[e]	Boatswain Mate 1/c 2833933	Died May 1999 (OH)
Whitworth Laurel "Woodie"	Ship's Cook 1/c 3599714	Died June 3, 1989

On the fates of the Filipino crew on the USS *Napa*, not much information can be found. Steward Bisente is known to have been killed in action; but of the other Stewards—Canilanza, Cenica, Gamoras, Larioza, Mendoza, Onkiko, Oquendo, Rapsing, and Reboja—nothing is known.

MINTER'S DOTING MOTHER, **Jou-Jou Dial,** turned ever more to her faith to help her live through the years after she lost her son. Living in DC after the war, she remained the matriarch of the family. She died May 12, 1960, at the age of eighty-two. She was survived by her two daughters, Fannie (1907–1998) and Dorothy (1909–2003), and her second son, Joseph (1914–1967).

Kennett Webb Hinks, Lisa's second husband and stepfather to her children, commissioned the small glass case that housed Minter's ring, Navy Cross, and Purple Heart. After serving as a senior executive for the J. Walter Thompson advertising agency, he retired to Ivy, Virginia. He was a devoted husband to Lisa and a man of great compassion, remembered by her children as "a steady rudder" and "a truly good man." He died in July 1982 at the age of eighty-five.

Diana Dial, Minter's daughter, still lives near her grand-mother's home in Washington, DC. She is inspired by the tale of her father's heroism and fortitude under such horrific circumstances, and she considers the story of the ring to be a miracle. Diana was touched by my efforts to discover all the details of her father's tale and was enthralled, but not surprised, by the intensity of her parents' love story. Diana admits that she feels a great yearning to have known her father and tries to conceal a bottomless sadness that seeing him again in this life is impossible. "There are characteristics that I have which might have come from him," she says. "I know that Aunt Fannie saw something in me that reminded her of her brother, my father, but I'm not sure exactly what she saw. So to this day I miss what I did not know." Diana still cries at mention of her father's death and found herself hoping that his spirit would watch over her son, Chris, a US Marine, as he completed his second tour in Iraq.

Victor Dial, Minter's son and my father, lives in Switzerland, retired from a career in the auto industry. Though reluctant at first, he came to take a deep interest in this book and began to share his reminiscences. From growing up attempting not to mention his father's name for fear of upsetting his mother and stirring up her unending grief, he became one of the driving forces behind celebrating Minter's memory, and actively supported the memorial to those who died aboard the hell ships—a permanent reminder of their suffering. I asked him to share what uncovering his father's story has meant to him. Here is what he wrote:

It was a typically warm and cloudless California day in July 1941, and my father was taking us for a drive in his beloved Lincoln Continental convertible. Mom was on the right, holding my baby sister in her lap, and I was squeezed in between. I loved driving in the car. We were on our way to the port because my father was going on a trip on a big boat and would be gone for a while.

After we parked the car, Daddy unloaded his bags, and we all walked together toward the quay where the huge ship was berthed. Suddenly my father swept me up into his strong arms and told me in his Southern Gentleman drawl that he was leaving for a new assignment and he'd be gone for a little while. I didn't like it when he left, and I began to cry, sad to see him go. My mother told me to be strong and brave, to show how much I loved my Daddy. He kissed my sister Diana, still in our mother's arms, and lastly he held my mother in a long embrace. Then he turned, and with a jaunty wave and a blown kiss, he boarded the ocean liner.

We stayed on the quay, along with the friends and family of other passengers, watching and waving until the ship sailed out of sight. I hoped he'd be back soon.

The foregoing scene is entirely made up, because I had just turned three, and I have no recollection at all of what actually took place when my father left, nor of anything at all about the time I spent with him. Nevertheless, it seems entirely plausible that his farewell happened pretty much as described. Sadly, my mother died in 1963, and I never had the wit to ask her about these matters prior to her death.

It saddens me to write that I don't think I missed my father as much as I should have. In my defense, it was hard to miss someone I'd hardly known and didn't remember. During the wartime years, I was fascinated by the planes and ships I saw offshore, and double features and cartoons and comic books, and learning how to body surf in the Pacific.

Sometime in 1946, my mother flew back to New York. It was time for a change of scene, and perhaps she hoped to plot a new life for her family. While she was away, Diana and I were left in the caring hands of our grandmother, living in her large house on the ocean in Long Beach, studying at the nearby James Russell Lowell Elementary School.

In New York, my mother stayed with Don Francisco and his wife Connie, her distinguished favorite cousin. Don introduced her to Kennett Hinks. They were married in New York in November 1946. After school was over in June, my mother flew back to

California and brought my sister and me to New York to meet our new stepfather and to begin a new life on the East Coast. If it was a big change for the three of us, it was an even bigger one for Kenn. One minute he was a carefree bachelor, the next he had a wife and two children, ages nine and seven. Not altogether surprisingly, our first years together were full of drama, quarrels, and imminent split-ups as the two sides adapted to their new lives. It was during these events that I saw for the first time a side of my mother that I didn't know, and that I began to realize the enormity of the tragedy that had befallen her.

In the fall of 1955, I had recently turned seventeen and was preparing to begin four years at Yale. The war in Korea had ended (sort of) two years before; but the draft still existed, and I would soon be reaching enlistable age. Students were being deferred, but that could change if the need arose. Talking with my parents, teachers, and friends, I decided that if I were to serve, it would be a far more valuable experience to be an officer than an enlisted man. Yale offered an ROTC (Reserve Officer Training Corps) program, and the Navy was an obvious slam-dunk choice. It meant that one of my five courses would have to be Navy ROTC, a six-week summer "cruise" between junior and senior year, and a two-year active duty commitment upon graduation.

The summer cruise was quite eventful. I was assigned to a destroyer (USS Kyes DD-787) based in Long Beach, as my father was so many years before. Shortly after reporting for duty, I was summoned to the bridge by the captain, a rare occurrence for a lowly midshipman. I hoped I hadn't done anything wrong. He handed me a message from the commanding officer of the USS Bryce Canyon (AD-36), Captain Archer, inviting me to lunch on board his ship. He sent his gig to pick me up and deliver me back. It turned out that the captain was a classmate of my father's at Annapolis. He asked me for news of my father, and of course I told him all I knew at that point. He was complimentary about my dad, as you would expect. When I returned to the Kyes in the captain's gig later on that afternoon, my fame among my fellow midshipmen had markedly improved. Things got less cushy after that: the Kyes was scheduled for maneuvers at sea, and we had to laboriously discharge our live ammunition for dumb ones. No sooner had this been completed when we got word of a fleet-wide alert due to a serious flare up in the Eastern Mediterranean. So we spent all night off-loading the dummy ammo and reloading the live stuff. Early the next morning, we promptly put out to sea as part of a group guarding the USS Midway. Only a few days later, we ran into the tail end of a typhoon south of Hawaii. Rough seas on a destroyer are challenging, and a typhoon is powerful. Many on board were seasick. I was a rare exception. Eventually the weather improved and things calmed down in Lebanon, so we proceeded with our scheduled exercises, acting as plane guard to the Midway while nighttime carrier landing qualifications took place. Unfortunately, two planes collided in mid-air and another crashed into the sea, so we spent many hours vainly searching first for survivors and then debris.

Upon graduation, I was commissioned an ensign in the US Naval Reserve and spent two interesting years headquartered at the US Naval Station in Algiers. Algiers, Louisiana, that is, just across the Mississippi River from New Orleans.

When my first son was born, my dear wife, Alix, readily agreed that he be named after my father, and that we'd also call him "Minter" (Minter was my grandmother's maiden name). When my son, Minter, started on his quest to find out more about his namesake more than twenty years ago, I wasn't much help. I guess my repressed memory was a sort of shield against further hurt. But I watched in admiration and amazement the energy and determination he devoted to finding out everything there was to know about his grandfather.

He traveled to annual reunions of surviving POWs of Bataan and Corregidor; he wrote letters, collected documents, made umpteen phone calls, and paid personal visits to find out all there was to know. He retraced Minter's travail from Corregidor to Bilibid, to Cabanatuan and back to Bilibid, to Pier 7 in Manila where the prisoners were crammed into the hold of the Oryoku Maru, and thence to Subic Bay where we thought my father had died on December 15, 1944. The conflicting stories told by survivors resulting in the confusion about the place and manner of Minter's death is a good example of the famous fog of war.

Minter's research has included reading and transcribing all the written records of Lisa and Minter's life together; finding and interviewing those who knew them; writing a manuscript of a book; writing a complete movie script; hiring a film director to produce a twenty-seven-minute film; maintaining second- and even third-generation family friendships; finding and interviewing fellow descendants of his fellow prisoners; finding and interviewing members of Minter's crew on the Napa; and many other lengths he went to in ferreting out information to tell my father's story.

I am in awe of the time and effort Minter has devoted to this project, because he's busy with so many other things in his rich life. I feel it has brought the two of us much closer together.

This project has helped me bring my father's life out from under the shadows of my mind, better understand my mother's suffering, and hope she has forgiven me my impatience with her.

In spite of my son's great work and the many years that have gone by, like Lisa, I'm not sure I will ever fully come to grips with the tragedy of the last years of my father's life, and what might have been.

Despite being the child of a member of the Greatest Generation, I never considered myself exceptional for having a war hero as a father. Though I came late to better understanding my father's bravery and sacrifice for his country, I am proud and humbled that he proved to be that type of man. He earned his place among that Greatest Generation, and I am thrilled to help my son tell his story. In a world too often stripped of honor and true courage, it is a story worth knowing.

– 12 –

STILL TOUCHING LIVES

A FTER THE *SMITHSONIAN* article about my grandfather and his ring was published in 2011, it was subsequently translated into Japanese and then published on the "US–Japan Dialogue on POWs" site, thanks to the help of Kinue Tokudome.[1]

Soon thereafter, I was contacted by a Japanese woman, Harumi Okuchi, a close friend of Haruku Ichimaru, the oldest daughter of Rinosuke Ichimaru, a renowned Navy pilot and rear admiral of the Japanese Imperial Navy.

Mrs. Okuchi shared a fascinating story with me after reading of my grandfather's ring.

In her initial letter to me, she wrote:

"I believe in Miracle [sic], because I myself have experienced. I was involved in a small project to find families and send back war souvenirs from Iwo Jima. I was very lucky and was able to find six cases in about six years. They were all miracles. These things happened because I wrote the story of Miracle Sword of Admiral Ichimaru, who died on Iwo Jima . . . ."

The story Okuchi told was of Haruku Ichimaru's father's sword, made by a renowned swordsmith during the Edo period and thought to contain the spirit of the samurai, the legendary warriors of ancient Japan. The admiral carried the sword throughout the war and used it to command his troops, but it was much more than ceremonial. The sword literally saved the admiral's life.

Once, while flying on a troop plane, the airplane came under attack. A bullet struck the admiral but hit the sword he was carrying, breaking off the tip, thus sparing Ichimaru's life. Mrs. Okuchi called this the "first miracle" associated with the sword. The sword was repaired, and Ichimaru served until the infamous Battle of Iwo Jima.

Admiral Ichimaru, along with his troops, was stationed on the island of Iwo Jima in August 1944, making defensive preparations. In March 1945, the Allies finally attacked the island, and Ichimaru died March 27, having left his cave. In the heat of battle, identifying bodies and places of burial was nigh on to impossible. So Haruko, the admiral's eldest daughter, who lived in Kyushu, made a wish that the unique saber would tell her where her father had fallen. But there was no news about the saber being found, and the admiral's body was lost forever.

The second miracle came twenty years later. A number of historians and surviving soldiers wrote retrospective books about the famed Battle of Iwo Jima. One of them, entitled *Iwo Jima* by Richard Newcomb and published in 1965, made mention of Ichimaru's sword. A history professor, Thomas Lane, who also fought as an eighteen-year-old Marine at Iwo Jima, read the book and wondered if the sword he'd bought for twenty-five dollars in a New Jersey flea market, labeled a "war souvenir from Iwo Jima," might be the admiral's sword. He researched the subject only to find it was indeed the missing sword. The professor arranged for the sword to be returned to the admiral's widow, Sueko, via a Japanese war veteran. He and Mrs. Ichimaru began a correspondence that culminated in a calligraphy poem inscribed on a fan thanking

Lane for returning the sword. The poem became one of Lane's most cherished possessions.

The widow allowed the sword to be displayed in Karatsu Castle Museum in a shrine in honor of her father. There, according to the chronicler, the third "miracle" happened. Five years after having donated the sword to the museum, there was a burglary, and the sword was stolen along with some other items on exhibition. Sueko had died in the intervening years, so Haruko, the eldest daughter, made another wish that the sword might come back to her. Three years later, a Japanese doctor, who bought a sword from an antique shop, researched the markings on it, a swordfish sign, and discovered it was the admiral's sword and duly returned it to Haruko, as she had wished.

She believed, for the rest of her life, that her father's spirit guarded her through the sword.

The parallels between this story and that of my grandfather's are stunning. Two naval officers, each of whom had an artifact of great personal significance lost during the war. These artifacts were both found, two decades later, in a totally different country than that in which they were lost. Having been found and returned to their owners, both were stolen five years later. Minter was taken prisoner, and Ichimaru was hit by a bullet at almost the same time. They would even die the same year, two months apart. The serendipity of timing is amazing. Not so surprising is that Haruko and I would both feel as though we were being watched over by the benevolent spirits of our heroic relatives. In her last message to me, Haruko (writing through Harumi) wished with all her heart that the ring should come back to us, as did her father's sword.

TELLING THE STORY of Minter's ring, as I have done so often now, does seem to inspire others to tell me their stories of what they have lost or sometimes found. My mother-in-law, Marguerite Sirieix, was born in 1929 in Eymoutiers, a small town some forty miles east of Limoges in what was known in WWII as Free

France. Her mother, Antoinette Sirieix Malavaud, told Marguerite throughout her life that her father had died several years prior to her birth, in 1921, after having been gassed in WWI. Even when she was old enough to realize that this story was impossible, Marguerite never questioned her mother until, stirred up by my writing of this book in which I searched for answers about my family, she took action to find out the truth about hers.

In the late 1990s, at seventy years old, Marguerite took it upon herself to return to her native town and inquire from its oldest residents if anyone had memories of her mother and a possible *special* male acquaintance around the time of her birth.

Because of her own investigation, Marguerite came back to tell us that she had found out who her genetic father had been. Moreover, she was able to track down Mme. Georgette Debord, the surviving daughter-in-law of her genetic father. This lady, frail and near ninety years old, was willing to meet with Marguerite and share mementos she had of Mr. Debord, Marguerite's true father.

Mr. Debord had been a respectable Notary Public from Limoges and a married man with two sons. He and Marguerite's mother had enjoyed a long affair before Debord died in 1931. Only one of his sons had ever married; they had no children. Theoretically, that meant that Marguerite was the only continuance of the Debord family line.

The search detailed in this book spurred Marguerite's search to find her father and her lineage and had done so just in the nick of time before the knowledge was lost with the death of Mme. Debord.

THIS BOOK DIDN'T just affect members of my extended family, however. I travel the world telling this story to many veteran, civic, and school groups. One session at a middle school at the Marymount School in Neuilly, France, brought out an emotion I never expected to bring forth from one of the ten-year-old audience members.

In the question-and-answer period following my presentation, where most questions came from eager boys wanting to know what it was like to die in a war and, less bloodthirsty, whether Minter's ring was ever found, one little girl kneeling in the front row had her hand in the air the whole time, though she never looked up at me.

I asked her what her question was, and, finally, she looked me in the eye, took a deep breath, and shared what was on her mind.

"Sir," she said, "I've never told anyone this before, but I'm adopted. Can you help me find out who my real parents are?"

Wishing I were in fact the Pied Piper of all lost things, even birth parents, I gently encouraged her to go home and speak to her adoptive parents about her birth parents. I didn't say out loud, but sincerely hoped her search for her birth parents would be as fulfilling as mine was for my grandfather.

WHILE I AM happy that my search has at least revealed the truth about Minter's life, there is still a sadness, not only at losing him the way we did, but for the men and women I missed speaking to before their passing, and for the years we seemed to have lost the memory of him. I was even slow to comprehend why I was doing this research. In a sign of this, when my son was born in 1997, I did not choose to follow the traditional Dial naming convention of Nathaniel X Dial, where X is the preferred forename, instead using only my mother's maiden name. Certainly, in retrospect, given what this family history has come to mean for me, I wonder at the gap. And, of course, there is a part of my quest that is still unfinished. My father and I still live in hope that one day, Minter's ring will be returned to his family, as Minter himself so dearly wished. We have tried every possible angle and appeal to make this happen, and while it has not yet paid off, we keep trying.

For example, around 1980, while living in France, my father befriended a renowned French journalist and Americanophile, Philippe Labro, and he brought up the theft of his father's ring.

Labro suggested organizing a nationwide campaign to get the public to help look for it. By chance a few days later, my father was invited to a very small duck shoot along with President Valéry Giscard d'Estaing. At lunch he told him about the ring and how it had been stolen in France. D'Estaing was moved by the story and, in honor of Franco-American friendship, thought the ring had to be returned! He told my father that if he developed a plan, he, D'Estaing, would support it. Sadly, a few weeks later, Giscard D'Estaing was defeated by François Mitterrand. Shortly thereafter, my father became occupied with a new and highly visible job at Peugeot, and the plan to mount a nationwide search sputtered out.

The *coup de grâce* for any such pipe dream came when the CEO of Renault, Georges Besse, was assassinated in 1986 by the Red Brigade. Aside from considering public appearances for such a personal story as an unnecessary risk in light of his role at Peugeot, there was the despondent feeling that the ring would never be found.

Victor's plan to recover his father's ring seemed to have come to a permanent halt. Until, that is, I received that telephone call out of the blue from Mrs. Chucker.

UNTIL THE RING returns to us, we have a space expressly waiting for it. Early in 2001, I had written to the Navy about the fact that my grandfather's Navy Cross and Purple Heart had been stolen. This involved sending sufficient paperwork to prove that they had been awarded to my grandfather and that I was his grandson. Without warning, in the early fall, we received two separate packages containing a genuine replacement of each medal. I was thrilled. When I opened them, I remember being surprised at the weight of the Navy Cross. It felt substantial in my hand.

In parallel, that summer, I had also contacted Bailey Banks & Biddle, the jeweler based out of Philadelphia that had originally made my grandfather's 1932 ring. Having found a way through to management, I was able to find someone willing to dig through the archives to uncover the original index card with the custom instructions for my grandfather's ring. They faxed the information over. Without hesitating, I commissioned a replica ring. Of course, it would be brand new and not bear the scars and markings, but it would be a handsome object.

With medals and ring in hand, I then found a charming picture framer, and, together, we devised a custom frame to house them. We included a picture of both my grandfather and grandmother. Laying everything on a rich burgundy velvet backdrop, bordered by a strong and elegant gold frame, we talked at length about the layout. The key idea was to include a purposeful space in the middle. This vacancy remains for when the original ring is returned.

It has been a long and magical journey for me, one which I love to share. I continue to travel the world telling students and groups the story of Nathaniel Minter Dial, war hero, father, and Southern Gentleman. I have produced a documentary film on the subject, *The Last Ring Home*,[2] to prevent this important piece of history from being lost and to honor the memory of those who gave their lives. I am asked constantly about the ring and have accepted countless good wishes that it should find its way back to us. The ring has taken on such an important role in my life that I sometimes feel it needs a name of its own. The name that I gave it was *Annapolisa*. May this book help to bring the Annapolisa ring back home at last.

— Endnotes —

CHAPTER 1
1. Hampton Sides, *Ghost Soldiers: The Epic Account of World War II's Greatest Rescue Mission* (New York: Doubleday, 2001), 132.
2. Conversation with Cmdr. John Schofield, Office of Public Affairs, USNA, Minter Dial II, US Naval Academy, Office of Public Relations, October 23, 2015.
3. Conversation with USNA PR Officer, US Naval Academy, Office of Public Relations, October 23, 2015.
4. Sides, *Ghost Soldiers*, 3.

CHAPTER 2
1. Margaret Mitchell, *Gone With the Wind* (New York: Macmillan, 1936).
2. Editorial, *Richmond Daily Dispatch*, March 11, 1861.
3. Sarah E. Hornady Chapter, UDC. Confederate Memorial, Schley County Courthouse. 1910. Marble. Monument. Ellaville, GA, November 1, 2015.
4. "Robert E Lee Quotes," Historynet, accessed April 24, 2016, http://www.historynet.com/robert-e-lee-quotes.
5. Life was fragile in the nineteenth century. On March 15, 1881, the author's great-great-grandmother, Fannie Dodson Minter née Ramseur, wife of John Russell Minter and sister to the gallant Maj. Gen. Stephen Dodson Ramseur, who died at the Battle of Cedar Creek in 1864. Fannie was seven months pregnant. Her ten-year-old daughter, also called Fannie, was warming up by the fire in the huge hearth when a gust of wind blew in from a door opening and made her dress catch fire. Little Fannie died right away. Her mother died of her burns ten days later. Josephine named her eldest daughter after Fannie.

6. Rebecca Dial, *True to his colors: A Story of South Carolina's Senator Nathaniel Barksdale Dial* (New York: Vantage Press, 1974).
7. Ibid.
8. Nathaniel wrote, "If you want your work to be like play, Just let the women have their way." Ibid., 135.
9. *Nathaniel Barksdale papers*, David M. Rubenstein Rare Book & Manuscript Library, Duke University, 1915, 1923–1935.
10. Dial, *True to his colors*.
11. Ibid.
12. Office of the Historian, United States House of Representatives. (n.d.). DIAL, Nathaniel Barksdale (1862–1940). Retrieved April 24, 2016, from Biographical Directory of the United States Congress: http://bioguide.congress.gov/scripts/biodisplay.pl?index=D000298.
13. "Senate Chamber Desks: Thomas Constantine, Cabinetmaker," US Senate, accessed April 24, 2016, http://www.senate.gov/artandhistory/art/special/Desks/hdetail.cfm?id=17.
14. "May 11, 1928: Senators Vote to Knock Out Walls," US Senate, accessed April 24, 2016, http://www.senate.gov/artandhistory/history/minute/Senators_Vote_To_Knock_Out_Walls.htm.
15. "The Seven Greatest Senators of All Time," accessed April 24, 2016, http://www.electoral-vote.com/evp2013/Info/greatest-senators.html.
16. From private papers and letters held by the author's family.
17. Ibid.
18. Ibid.
19. Jerry L. Slaunwhite, "The Public Career of Nathaniel Barksdale Dial" (Ph.D. diss., University of South Carolina, 1979).
20. V. Dial, "The Speech That Never Was," unpublished research paper.
21. Dial, *True to his colors*.
22. Ibid.

CHAPTER 3
1. In 1930, the Association of American Universities accredited the Naval Academy, and in 1933, an act of Congress authorized the Naval Academy to confer the degree of bachelor of science on graduates, beginning with the Class of 1931 ("USNA ViewBook," United States Naval Academy, last modified 2014, http://www.usna.edu/Viewbook/_files/documents/USNA-Viewbook.pdf).
2 Ibid.
3. Ibid.
4. "Honor Concept," United States Naval Academy, accessed April 23, 2016, http://www.usna.edu/About/honorconcept.php.

5. Corky Ward would end up a four-star admiral. ("Admiral Corky Ward," Battleship North Carolina Collections Online, accessed April 24, 2016, http://battleshipnc.pastperfectonline.com/photo/F076F9C4-2CB1-11D9-8AD3-008928053500.

6. "2009 Navy Lacrosse Media Guide," Navy Sports, last modified 2009, http://www.navysports.com/sports/m-lacros/spec-rel/09-media-guide.html.

7. The original bell, donated to the Naval Academy by Commodore Perry's widow, was returned by the Navy to the people of Okinawa in 1987. Like the original bell, the replica is rung to celebrate football victories over Army.

8. "USNA Viewbook."

9. Copy of USNA 1932 commencement speech provided by James W. Cheever, senior curator, US Naval Academy Museum.

10. The 1932 German presidential elections were held on March 13. The incumbent resident, Paul von Hindenburg, was reelected to a second term of office. His major opponent in the election was Adolf Hitler of the Nazi Party. Hindenburg played an important role in the coming to power of the Nazis, reluctantly appointing Hitler as chancellor of Germany in January 1933.

CHAPTER 4

1. Mrs. Porter's School for Girls was located at 1256 East Ocean Blvd. It was a day school, established in 1914, for girls ages four to seventeen. Principal tuition was recorded as one hundred fifty dollars, or more than three thousand five hundred in current dollars.

2. Norman Friedman, *U.S. Battleships: An Illustrated Design History* (Annapolis: Naval Institute Press, 1985).

3. "Arizona Afloat as 75,000 Cheer," *New York Times*, 1915.

4. Robert Patterson, the father of my aunt Ginger Mongomery (on my mother's side), became Secretary of War under President Truman and played a huge role in ramping up military production prior to and during the war. See Keith E. Eiler, *Mobilizing America: Robert P. Patterson and the War Effort, 1940–1945* (Ithaca: Cornell University Press, 1997).

CHAPTER 5

1. All letter excerpts from unpublished letters collected by the author's family.

2. All first-hand accounts from the USS *Napa* crew in this chapter as recounted to the author in interviews. This quote is from William Wells.

3. As recounted to the author by John Oleksa.

4. As recounted to the author by Harold Richardson.

5. As recounted to the author by William Bagwell.

6. As recounted to the author by Harold Richardson.

7. "Sub Raid in Self Defense, Say Nazis," *Standard-Examiner*, September 6, 1941.

8. "U.S. Denies Greer Attacker," *Waterloo Sunday Courier*. September 7, 1941, 1.
9. President Roosevelt made thirty fireside chats between 1933 and 1944. These were made in the form of radio addresses and represented a bold new form of communication for the chief executive to talk directly to the public.
10. Franklin D. Roosevelt, "Fireside Chat 18: On The Greer Incident," Miller Center of Public Affairs, University of Virginia, September 11, 1941, http://millercenter.org/scripps/archive/speeches/detail/3323.
11. Ibid.
12. Ibid.
13. Maurice Matloff and Edwin M. Snell, *Strategic Planning for Coalition Warfare, 1941–1942* (Washington, DC: Center of Military History, United States Army, 1953).
14. Michael Gough, "Failure and Destruction: Clark Field, the Philippines, December 8, 1941," *Military History Online*, November 2007, http://www.militaryhistoryonline.com/wwii/articles/failureanddestruction.aspx#.
15. William Manchester, *American Caesar: Douglas MacArthur 1880-1964* (New York: Little, Brown & Company, 1978).
16. Gough, "Failure and Destruction."
17. Ibid.
18. William H. Bartsch. *December 8, 1941: MacArthur's Pearl Harbor* (College Station: Texas A&M University Press, 2003).
19. In fact, there were a total of eighty-eight Japanese warplanes en route to hit various targets.

CHAPTER 6
1. Minter often wrote that his wife lacked confidence.
2. In the fall of 1943, after almost two years at war, concerns about public complacency led government officials to begin to allow the publication of images that showed the true cost of war. In the September 20, 1943, issue of *LIFE* magazine, the editors published a photograph taken on a New Guinea beach in the South Pacific ten months earlier. It was the first image of dead American servicemen that American civilians were allowed to see in the twenty-one months since Pearl Harbor.
3. PBS, "Communication: News and Censorship," *The War* documentary webpage, last modified September 2007, https://www.pbs.org/thewar/at_home_communication_news_censorship.htm.

CHAPTER 7
1. The SS *Corregidor* was sunk by a "friendly" mine, with five hundred killed trying to get out of the bay.
2. Sides, *Ghost Soldiers*, 42.

3. One of four tunnels used by the Navy within Malinta Hill.

4. Sides, *Ghost Soldiers*, 36.

5. "It was the dry season in the Philippines, and the lack of rain, choking dust storms, temperatures usually above ninety degrees, and near 100-percent humidity made for an unpleasant environment..." See Richard Sassaman, "The Battling Bastards of Bataan," *America in WWII*, April 2007, http://www.americainwwii.com/articles/the-battling-bastards-of-bataan/.

6. To make matters worse, the Filipinos' weapons and munitions dated from World War I. Only one in three mortar shells would explode, and maybe one in five hand grenades. Many rifles had broken extractors, so after each bullet was fired, the shell case had to be pushed out of the gun with a piece of bamboo. The more modern M-1 rifles "became highly undependable" when dirty, said one private. "We got tired of pulling the trigger and having nothing happen." Ibid.

7. Marconi M. Dioso, *The Times When Men Must Die: The Story of the Destruction of the Philippine Army During the Early Months of World War II in the Pacific, December 1941–May 1942* (Pittsburgh: Dorrance Publishing Co., Inc., 2010).

8. Gerald Flurry, "Did America Betray MacArthur and the Filipinos?," *The Trumpet* 9, no. 10, December 1998.

9. Sides, *Ghost Soldiers*, 42.

10. Hanson W. Baldwin, "The Fourth Marines at Corregidor," *Marine Corps Gazette* 30, issue 11 (1946): 13.

11. Sassaman, "The Battling Bastards of Bataan."

12. "Fighting On," from *Nothing But Praise*, the posthumous collection of Lee's poetry collected from his buried journal. See Henry Garnsey Lee, *Nothing But Praise* (Culver City, CA: Murray & Gee, 1948).

13. Louis Morton, *The Fall of the Philippines* (Washington, DC: Center of Military History, United States Army, 1953), 464.

14. There were three other islands in Manila Bay, including Carabao, Fort Drum, and Fort Hughes, the latter of which was run by Cdr. Francis Bridget, who plays a part in the unfolding story. Commander Bridget assumed command of the beach defenses during the Philippines Campaign with eight hundred men under his command. See "Corregidor—Then and Now: The Harbor Defenses of Manila Bay," accessed April 24, 2016, http://corregidor.org/Corregidor Resources/53-63678/under_siege_lm1a_composite.htm.

15. Sides, *Ghost Soldiers*, 41.

16. Dana Rohrabacher, "Paying Homage to a Special Group of Veterans, Survivors of Bataan and Corregidor," *Congressional Record—House* 147, no. 90, 11980–11985.

17. Shannon E. French, *The Code of the Warrior: Exploring Warrior Values Past and Present* (New York: Rowman and Littlefield, 2003), 222.

18. Holly Senatore, "Bushido: The Valor of Deceit," Military History Online, March 29, 2009: http://www.militaryhistoryonline.com/wwii/articles/bushido.aspx#.

19. Ibid.

20. The death toll varies because it is unclear to historians how many prisoners, especially Filipinos, escaped to blend in with the civilian population along the way.

21. Sides, *Ghost Soldiers*, 91.

22. Regarding Malta, I found a passage written in *LIFE* magazine, May 4, 1942 (ironically a couple of days before the surrender of Corregidor).
    In the article, they wrote:

    > "The most heavily bombed spot in the world is not London or Chungking or Tobruk or Corregidor but a little British island in mid-Mediterranean. Malta, 8 miles wide and 17 miles long, has been bombed more than 2,000 times. It has the heaviest concentration per area of anti-aircraft guns in the world, on land and on board ship. Between 150 to 200 Axis planes strike at this British carbuncle in Mussolini's sea every 24 hours."

23. Duane Schultz, *Hero of Bataan: The Story of General Jonathan M. Wainwright* (New York: St. Martin's Press, 1981).

24. Cdr. M.H. McCoy, later rear admiral, from El Paso, Texas, wrote Lisa a letter dated April 4, 1944, in which he detailed Minter's "excellent health" and McCoy's surety that Minter would survive his imprisonment.

25. John M. Wright Jr, *Captured on Corregidor: Diary of an American POW in World War II* (Jefferson, NC: McFarland & Co, 1988), 93.

26. As Harold "Richie" Richardson (who served on the *Napa* and was in Cabanatuan Camp No. 1 with Minter) recounted to the author.

27. As recounted to the author by John Oleksa.

28. "The March of Death," *Bureau of Naval Personnel Information Bulletin* (March 1994), 26.

29. Excerpts from an autobiographical article, written by two prisoners who escaped from Davao, for the February 7, 1944, edition of *LIFE* Magazine, give a vivid insight. Of the ten men who escaped, eight were said to make it home. It took some six months of hiding and daring submarine rescue to get the men to Australia, where they debriefed General MacArthur. These men finally brought the truth home about the defense of Bataan and Corregidor, the Bataan Death March, and the mistreatment of the men in Cabanatuan and elsewhere.

30. As recounted to the author by Ken Wheeler.

31. From the diary of Meade H. Willis Jr.

32. As recounted to the author by Harold Richardson.

33. Robert S. LaForte, Ronald E. Marcello, and Richard Himmel, *With Only Will to Live: Accounts of Americans in Japanese Prison Camps 1941–1945* (New York: Rowman & Littlefield, 1994), 29.

34. Sides, *Ghost Soldiers*, 107.

35. Duane Heisinger, *Father Found: Life and Death as a Prisoner of the Japanese in World War II* (Maitland, FL: Xulon Press, 2003), 262.

36. Gavan Daws, *Prisoners of the Japanese: POWs of World War II in the Pacific* (New York: William Morrow & Company, 1996), 105.

37. The Navy Cross is not handed out liberally. A total of 3,972 Navy Crosses were awarded to 3,634 separate individuals for heroism in WWII, of which 2,897 went to members of the US Navy. The Navy Cross is the second highest military decoration, behind the Congressional Medal of Honor. "There weren't many citations handed out, it's true. As one officer wryly remarked, 'Losers don't get medals.' There were many more decorations handed out later in the war as the US Navy reconquered the Pacific and elsewhere. See Daws, *Prisoners of the Japanese*, 57.

38. The USS *Napa* was awarded one battle star for her service in World War II.

39. "Wife Hears Husband on Corregidor," *The Press Telegram*, May 5, 1942.

40. "Lieutenant Dial on Corregidor, Mother is Told," *Greenville Daily* (Greenville, SC), April 11, 1942.

41. By then, the Japanese had more important things on which to concentrate. MacArthur was pressing on the northern tip of New Guinea.

42. The author obtained this information from the diary of Meade Willis in his possession.

43. Dominic J. Caraccilo, editor, *Surviving Bataan and Beyond: Colonel Irvin Alexander's Odyssey as a Japanese Prisoner of War* (New York: Stackpole Books, 1999).

44. The "all my love" portion of this sentence was undoubtedly true. That he weighed 205 pounds was undoubtedly not. Before the war, he weighed 190 pounds.

45. Note that the option "uninjured" on the Red Cross POW cards becomes "injured" on the November 23, 1943, card. In all evidence, the only choice to be made was "not under treatment." Otherwise, the card would be censored. In this card, there were three "bad" choices versus one "passing" grade. Given the paucity of words, one can imagine that much was read into small changes in wording.

46. Ruffin recounted this story to me personally when I visited him in 1991. As he recollected the events, tears began streaming down his cheeks. His voice began to waver. He took a deep breath and continued reading, his Southern accent getting stronger as he read. The makeshift Cabanatuan prison camp library had an edition of *John Brown's Body* printed in Garden City, the same edition Minter had in his home library. Lisa would not be parted from that book for the rest of her life.

CHAPTER 8

1. Sides, *Ghost Soldiers*, 159–62.

2. Ibid., 202.

3. Ibid., 203.

4. Caraccilo, *Surviving Bataan and Beyond*.
5. Betty B. Jones, *The December Ship: A Story of Lt. Col. Arden R. Boellner's Capture in the Philippines, Imprisonment, and Death on a World War II Japanese Hellship* (Jefferson, NC: McFarland & Company, Inc., 1992).
6. The reference to the passage in *John Brown's Body*.
7. Sides, *Ghost Soldiers*, 204–5.
8. Ibid.
9. Ibid.
10. Ibid. 206.
11. Capt. Francis J Bridget died January 28, 1945, on board the *Brazil Maru* and was buried at sea. He was awarded the Navy Cross and Legion of Merit.
12. Of the 1,619 prisoners, two-thirds were officers: ninety-two lieutenant colonels, 170 majors, 261 army and marine captains, five commanders, fourteen lieutenant commanders (including Jack Littig), thirty-six naval lieutenants (among them Minter, Warwick Scott, Douglas Fisher, Shields Goodman), four hundred army lieutenants, twelve naval lieutenants (junior grade) (including Ken Wheeler), and thirty-one ensigns (including Perroneau Wingo).
13. Charles M. Brown et al., "The Oryoko Maru Story," *The Oryoko Maru Online*, 1983, http://www.oryokumaruonline.org/oryoku_maru_story.html.
14. The National Archives, "Littig, John C." See bibliography.
15. Sides, *Ghost Soldiers*, 213.
16. Fr. Cummings was the originator of the famous observation, "There are no atheists in foxholes," from one of his Bataan field sermons. See Donald R. McClarey, "Give Us This Day," *The American Catholic*, August 8, 2011.
17. Sidney Stewart, *Give Us This Day* (New York: W. W. Norton & Company, 1957), 203–4.
18. Michael Hurst, "The Story of the Bombing of the Enoura Maru," Taiwan POW Camps Memorial Society, January 9, 1945, http://www.powtaiwan.org/archives_detail.php?THE-STORY-OF-THE-BOMBING-OF-THE-ENOURA-MARU-17.
19. January 9, 1945, is listed on Minter's Official Death Certificate, filed with the US Navy, which was originated by the Japanese, although no Japanese medical officer's name or seal was given. The death certificate is dated January 10, 1947. Cause of death was cited as "Died in bombing." Name of illness: "Bomb fragment wounds in the dorsal region." Place of death: *Enoura Maru*.
20. Sides, *Ghost Soldiers*, 214.
21. William Chalek, *Guest of the Emperor* (New York: Writers Club Press, 2002), 205.
22. C. Brian Kelly and I. Smyer, *Best Little Stories from World War II* (Naperville, IL: Sourcebooks, Inc., 2010), 340.

CHAPTER 9

1. Duane Heisinger is the author of a great read, *Father Found*, published by Xulon Press in 2003.
2. These documents, declassified by Executive Order 13526 on December 29, 2009, were brought to my attention by Bob Hudson, a fellow researcher, in early 2016.
3. This text is a transcription of a tape recording of Cmdr. Douglas Fisher, kindly passed on to me by his stepson, John Littig Jr. It was transcribed in the mid-1960s.

CHAPTER 10

1. In addition to the Navy Cross and Purple Heart (awarded posthumously) mentioned above, Minter was given the American Defense Service Medal, Fleet Clasp, the Asiatic-Pacific Area Campaign Medal, the Army Distinguished Unit Badge, and the Philippine Defense Campaign Ribbon.

CHAPTER 11

1. Figures from AXPOW Association, March 15, 2000, http://lindavdahl.com/ FrontPage_Links/pows_of_the_japanese.htm, research by Charles A. Stenger, Ph.D., for the Department of Veterans Affairs, veteran of WWII, former POW of the European theater, and member of the Secretary's Committee on Former Prisoners of War.
2. Martin Gilbert, *The Second World War: A Complete History* (New York: Henry Holt and Company, 2004), 746.
3. John W. Dower, *Embracing Defeat* (New York: W.W. Norton & Company, 1999).
4. More information about the original ADBC is available at http://philippine-defenders.lib.wv.us/html/history.html. There is now an American Defenders of Bataan and Corregidor Memorial Society, the mission of which is to perpetuate the story of the bravery and sacrifice of the men and women who were thrown into the maelstrom of war in the early part of World War II. http:// www.dg-adbc.org/.
5. Office of the Historian, United States House of Representatives. (n.d.). COX, William Ruffin (1831–1919). Retrieved April 26, 2016, from Biographical Directory of the United States Congress: http://bioguide.congress.gov/scripts/ biodisplay.pl?index=c000841.
6. "Hall of Valor: William Ruffin Cox," *Military Times*, accessed April 26, 2016. http://valor.militarytimes.com/recipient.php?recipientid=19041.
7. Gilbert King, "Minter's Ring: The Story of One World War II POW," *Smithsonian. com*, Aug. 2, 2011, http://www.smithsonianmag.com/history/minters-ring-the-story-of-one-world-war-ii-pow-40301808/?no-ist.

8. Max Lancaster West was awarded a Silver Star for gallantry in action as a member of the beach defenses of Corregidor on May 2, 1942.

CHAPTER 12
1. In Japanese: http://www.us-japandialogueonpows.org/Dial-J.htm. In English: http://www.us-japandialogueonpows.org/Dial.htm.
2. http://thelastringhome.com

— Bibliography —

Baldwin, Hanson W. "The Fourth Marines at Corregidor." *Marine Corps Gazette* 30, issue 11 (1946): 13.

Bartsch, William H. *December 8, 1941: MacArthur's Pearl Harbor.* College Station: Texas A&M University Press, 2003.

Battleship North Carolina Collections Online. "Admiral Corky Ward." Accessed April 24, 2016. http://battleshipnc.pastperfectonline.com/photo/F076F9C4-2CB1-11D9-8AD3-008928053500

Biographical Directory of the United Stated Congress. "Cox, William Ruffin (1831–1919)." Accessed April 26, 2016. http://bioguide.congress.gov/scripts/biodisplay.pl?index=c000841

Biographical Directory of the United Stated Congress. "Dial, Nathaniel Barksdale (1862–1940)." Accessed April 24, 2016. http://bioguide.congress.gov/scripts/biodisplay.pl?index=D000298

Brown, Charles M., Loyd E. Mills, Edward Konik, Arthur G. Beale, and Edward Fisher. "The Oryoko Maru Story." *The Oryoko Maru Online.* 1983. http://www.oryokumaruonline.org/oryoku_maru_story.html

Caraccilo, Dominic J., ed. *Surviving Bataan and Beyond: Colonel Irvin Alexander's Odyssey as a Japanese Prisoner of War.* New York: Stackpole Books, 1999.

Chalek, William. *Guest of the Emperor.* New York: Writers Club Press, 2002.

Corregidor.org. "Corregidor—Then and Now: The Harbor Defenses of Manila Bay." Accessed April 24, 2016. http://corregidor.org/CorregidorResources/53-63678/under_siege_lm1a_composite.htm

Daws, Gavan. *Prisoners of the Japanese: POWs of World War II in the Pacific.* New York: William Morrow & Company, 1996.

Dial, Rebecca. *True to his colors: A Story of South Carolina's Senator Nathaniel Barksdale Dial.* New York: Vantage Press, 1974.

Dial, Victor. *The Speech That Never Was.* Unpublished.

Dioso, Marconi M. *The Times When Men Must Die: The Story of the Destruction of the Philippine Army During the Early Months of World War 11 in the Pacific, December 1941–May 1942.* Pittsburgh: Dorrance Publishing Co., Inc., 2010.

Dower, John W. *Embracing Defeat.* New York: W. W. Norton & Company, 1999.

Eiler, Keith E. *Mobilizing America: Robert P. Patterson and the War Effort, 1940–1945.* Ithaca: Cornell University Press, 1997.

Electoral Vote. "The Seven Greatest Senators of All Time." Accessed April 24, 2016. http://www.electoral-vote.com/evp2013/Info/greatest-senators.html

Flurry, Gerald. "Did America Betray MacArthur and the Filipinos?" *The Trumpet* 9, no. 10, December 1998.

French, Shannon E. *The Code of the Warrior: Exploring Warrior Values Past and Present.* New York: Rowman and Littlefield, 2003.

Friedman, Norman. *U.S. Battleships: An Illustrated Design History.* Annapolis: Naval Institute Press, 1986.

Gilbert, Martin. *The Second World War: A Complete History.* New York: Henry Holt and Company, 2004, 746.

Gough, Michael. "Failure and Destruction: Clark Field, the Philippines, December 8, 1941." *Military History Online.* November 2007. http://www.militaryhistory online.com/wwii/articles/failureanddestruction.aspx#

Hanlon, Christopher. "Puritans vs. Cavaliers." Disunion, *New York Times.* January 24, 2013. http://opinionator.blogs.nytimes.com/2013/01/24/puritans-vs-cavaliers/

Heisinger, Duane. *Father Found: Life and Death as a Prisoner of the Japanese in World War 11.* Maitland, FL: Xulon Press, 2003.

Historynet. "Robert E Lee Quotes." Accessed April 24, 2016. http://www.history-net.com/robert-e-lee-quotes

Hurst, Michael. "The Story of the Bombing of the *Enoura Maru.*" *Taiwan POW Camps Memorial Society.* January 9, 1945. http://www.powtaiwan.org/archives_detail.php?THE-STORY-OF-THE-BOMBING-OF-THE-ENOURA-MARU-17

Jones, Betty B. *The December Ship: A Story of Lt. Col. Arden R. Boellner's Capture in the Philippines, Imprisonment, and Death on a World War 11 Japanese Hellship.* Jefferson, NC: McFarland & Company, Inc., 1992.

Kelly, C. Brian, & I. Smyer. *Best Little Stories from World War 11.* Naperville, IL: Sourcebooks, Inc., 2010.

King, Gilbert. "Minter's Ring: The Story of One World War 11 POW." *Smithsonian. com.* August 2, 2011. http://www.smithsonianmag.com/history/minters-ring-the-story-of-one-world-war-ii-pow-40301808/?no-ist

LaForte, Robert S., Ronald E. Marcello, and Richard Himmel. *With Only Will to Live: Accounts of Americans in Japanese Prison Camps 1941-1945*. New York: Rowman & Littlefield, 1994.

Lee, Henry Garnsey. *Nothing But Praise*. Culver City, CA: Murray & Gee, 1948.

"Lieutenant Dial on Corregidor, Mother is Told." *Greenville Daily* (Greenville, SC), April 11, 1942.

Manchester, William. *American Caesar: Douglas MacArthur 1880-1964*. New York: Little, Brown & Company, 1978.

"The March of Death." Bureau of Naval Personnel Information Bulletin, p. 26. March 1994.

Matloff, Maurice, and Edwin M. Snell. *Strategic Planning for Coalition Warfare, 1941-1942*. Washington, DC: Center of Military History, United States Army, 1953.

McClarey, Donald R. "Give Us This Day." *The American Catholic*. August 8, 2011. http://the-american-catholic.com/2011/08/08/give-us-this-day/

Military Times. "Hall of Valor: William Ruffin Cox." Accessed April 26, 2016. http://valor.militarytimes.com/recipient.php?recipientid=19041

Mitchell, Margaret. *Gone with the Wind*. New York: Macmillan, 1936.

Morton, Louis. *The Fall of the Philippines*. Washington, DC: Center of Military History, United States Army, 1953.

Nathaniel Barksdale papers. David M. Rubenstein Rare Book & Manuscript Library, Duke University, 1915, 1923-1935.

The National Archives. "Littig, John C." Archives.gov. Accessed April 26, 2016. https://aad.archives.gov/aad/record-detail.jsp?dt=466&mtch=1&cat=alL&Tf=F&Sc=11675,11660,11679,11667,11669,11676,11672,11673&bc=sl,fD&Txt_11660=John+C.+LittiG&Op_11660=0&nfo_11660=V,24,1900&rpp=10&pg=1&rid=34850

Navy Sports. "2009 Navy Lacrosse Media Guide." http://www.navysports.com/sports/m-lacros/spec-rel/09-media-guide.html

New York Times. "Arizona Afloat as 75,000 Cheer." June 20, 1915.

PBS. "Communication: News and Censorship." *The War* documentary webpage. September 2007. https://www.pbs.org/thewar/at_home_communication_news_censorship.htm

Editorial. *Richmond Daily Dispatch*. (1861, March 11). *The Daily Dispatch*.

Rohrabacher, Dana. "Paying Homage to a Special Group of Veterans, Survivors of Bataan and Corregidor." *Congressional Record—House* 147, no. 90, pp. 11980-11985. Washington, DC: US House of Representatives.

Roosevelt, Franklin D. "Fireside Chat 18: On The Greer Incident." Miller Center of Public Affairs, University of Virginia, September 11, 1941. http://millercenter.org/scripps/archive/speeches/detail/3323

Sassaman, Richard. "The Battling Bastards of Bataan." *America in WWII*, April 2007. http://www.americainwwii.com/articles/the-battling-bastards-of-bataan/

Schultz, Duane. *Hero of Bataan: The Story of General Jonathan M. Wainwright.* New York: St. Martin's Press, 1981.

Senatore, Holly. "Bushido: The Valor of Deceit." *Military History Online*, March 29, 2009: http://www.militaryhistoryonline.com/wwii/articles/bushido.aspx#

Sides, Hampton. Ghost Soldiers: *The Epic Account of World War II's Greatest Rescue Mission.* New York: Doubleday, 2001.

Slaunwhite, Jerry L. "The Public Career of Nathaniel Barksdale Dial." Ph.D. diss., University of South Carolina, 1979.

Stewart, Sidney. *Give Us This Day.* New York: W. W. Norton & Company, 1957.

"Sub Raid in Self Defense, Say Nazis." *Standard-Examiner.* September 6, 1941.

"U.S. Denies Greer Attacker." *Waterloo Sunday Courier*, 1. September 7, 1941

United States Naval Academy. "2014 USNA Viewbook." Last modified 2014. http://www.usna.edu/Viewbook/_files/documents/USNA-Viewbook.pdf

United States Naval Academy. "Honor Concept." Accessed April 23, 2016. http:// www.usna.edu/About/honorconcept.php

US Senate. "May 11, 1928: Senators Vote to Knock Out Walls." Accessed April 24, 2016. http://www.senate.gov/artandhistory/history/minute/Senators_Vote_To_Knock_Out_Walls.htm

US Senate. "Senate Chamber Desks: Thomas Constantine, Cabinetmaker." Accessed April 24, 2016. http://www.senate.gov/artandhistory/art/special/Desks/hdetail.cfm?id=17

"Wife Hears Husband on Corregidor." *The Press Telegram.* May 5, 1942.

Wright, John M., Jr. *Captured on Corregidor: Diary of an American POW in World War II.* Jefferson, NC: McFarland & Co, 1988.

— Acknowledgments —

M<small>ANY PEOPLE HAVE</small> helped me along the way in my research, in compiling the facts, facilitating contacts, and connecting the dots. Of the hundreds of World War II veterans I have interviewed or met during the past twenty-five years, I fear most have since passed away. To their spirits, I send my eternal gratitude. To their descendants, I send an open invitation to stay in touch.

Meanwhile, among the many friends and connections who have helped, I would like to thank in particular: Randy Anderson, Edna Binkowski, Jim Cheevers (USNA), Sasha Gifford, Kevin Hamdorf, Tudy Hill, Robert Hudson, Gilbert King, Mindy Kotler, Steve Kwiecinski, John Littig Jr., Adam Minakowski (USNA), Fred Stahl, Naoshi Takatsu, Jan Thompson, Terry Thompson, Kinue Tokudome, Timothy Woodbury (USNA), and Margy Wooding.

I would also like to thank the great team at Page Two—Trena, Megan, Helen, Peter, and Kristen—for their invaluable support and help.

Finally, turning to my family, this project could not have been achieved without the fabulous support and inputs from my cousins Matthew Perry, Rob Perry, and Chris Noone; my aunt Diana Dial (guardian of all the archives); my mother, Alix Estey (for all the encouragement, editing, and advice); the unending support of my beautiful wife, Yendi, and our two children, Oscar and Alexandra, who have had to listen to the story countless times over the years; and, of course, my father, Victor Dial, for whom and with whom this book and this story have been made.

If you would like to request more information about this story, correct inaccuracies, provide feedback, or simply get in touch, please email TLRH@myndset.com.

— Index —